The Complete Guide for THE ANXIOUS BRIDE

How to Avoid Everything That Could Go Wrong on Your Big Day

LEAH INGRAM

New Page Books
A division of Career Press, Inc.
Franklin Lakes, NJ

Copyright © 2004 by Leah Ingram

All rights reserved under the Pan-American and International Copyright Conventions. This book may not be reproduced, in whole or in part, in any form or by any means electronic or mechanical, including photocopying, recording, or by any information storage and retrieval system now known or hereafter invented, without written permission from the publisher, The Career Press.

THE COMPLETE GUIDE FOR THE ANXIOUS BRIDE
EDITED AND TYPESET BY KATE HENCHES
Cover design by Cheryl Cohan Finbow
Cover Photograph by Gary Jung
Printed in the U.S.A. by Book-mart Press

To order this title, please call toll-free 1-800-CAREER-1 (NJ and Canada: 201-848-0310) to order using VISA or MasterCard, or for further information on books from Career Press.

The Career Press, Inc., 3 Tice Road, PO Box 687,
Franklin Lakes, NJ 07417
www.careerpress.com
www.newpagebooks.com

Library of Congress Cataloging-in-Publication Data

Ingram, Leah.
 The complete guide for the anxious bride : how to avoid everything that could go wrong on your big day / by Leah Ingram.
   p. cm.
 Includes index.
 ISBN 1-56414-730-4 (pbk.)
  1. Weddings—Planning—Miscellanea. 2. Problem solving. I. Title.

HQ745.I64 2004
395.2′2--dc22

2003070216

Dedication

*To Bill, Jane, and Annie.
And to all the brides who are anxious
about their wedding:
Close your eyes, take a deep breath, exhale, open
your eyes, and start reading.*

 # Acknowledgments

My husband is a partner in my writing business by providing love, support, and inspiration for all of the work I do. He also feeds and bathes the kids and puts them to bed whenever I'm on deadline. So if it wasn't for him, I couldn't have written this book. Thank you, Bill.

Thank you also to the terrific trio of agents at Sheree Bykofsky and Associates: Janet Rosen, Megan Buckley, and Sheree Bykofsky. This book was our first project together, and you three pros continued to believe in this book's potential when no one else did. Well, you were right—and here it is, getting published.

Furthermore, thank you to my cousin Cara, who allowed me to give her unlimited and sometimes unsolicited advice as she planned her wedding this past fall. By allowing me to get back inside the mind of an anxious bride (although you were pretty calm, Cara—probably all that meditating and yoga that you do), you made writing this book much easier.

Finally, thank you to all the "anxious brides" out there who shared their sob stories, wedding disasters, and special-event snafus. Without your real-life anecdotes, I never would have known exactly how many things could possibly go wrong on a wedding day. I found all of you through friends and family members, and services such as Profnet, Freelance Success, and the American Society of Journalists and Authors' online phorum. Therefore, I must send a big thanks out to each of these services and the help they provided me in researching and writing this book.

Contents

Introduction   9

Chapter 1: Health Concerns   11

Ill-timed period ❦ unplanned pregnancy ❦ bride and groom got sick ❦ broken bones ❦ under-the-weather wedding party ❦ ill parents.

Chapter 2: Beauty Emergencies   23

Acne breakout ❦ bride with braces ❦ missing contact lenses ❦ lost or broken glasses ❦ oral surgery ❦ unexpected sunburn ❦ unavailable hairdresser and makeup artist ❦ switching stylists ❦ fake nails gone bad ❦ toupees and comb-overs.

Chapter 3: Sticky Situations   35

Vendors demanding cash ❦ bounced checks ❦ overextended budget ❦ over-the-top bachelor party ❦ secrets revealed on video ❦ pushy parents ❦ negotiating divorced parents ❦ inviting work colleagues ❦ getting fired.

Chapter 4: Bridal Gown and Groom's Attire   49

Missing wedding gown ❦ tips for getting a gown in a pinch ❦ wedding dress damaged ❦ dress doesn't fit ❦ hate the dress you ordered ❦ can't get tuxedos.

Chapter 5: Wedding Accessories and Bridesmaid Attire   65

Shoes that hurt ❦ missing undergarments ❦ panty lines ❦ bridesmaid dresses not ready ❦ bridesmaid dresses all wrong ❦ maternity bridesmaid attire ❦ color wars ❦ cheapskate attendants ❦ tuxes don't fit.

Chapter 6: The Wedding Party   75

Attendants want out ❦ pregnant bridesmaid ❦ fighting attendants ❦ firing an attendant ❦ problems with flower girl and ring bearer ❦ married attendants that split up.

Chapter 7: The Wedding Ceremony   87

Bad weather ❦ ceremony location unavailable ❦ parents insist on religious ceremony ❦ officiant overbooked ❦ ceremony site too small ❦ officiant is a low talker ❦ two religions in one ceremony ❦ ceremony locale is too hot/too cold ❦ dealing with daylight savings ❦ church is noisy ❦ collapsing huppah ❦ broken glass.

Chapter 8: The Entertainment   109

Avoiding bad performers ❦ reception band broke up ❦ unavailable entertainer ❦ loud band ❦ bandleader/deejay obnoxious ❦ song list all wrong.

Chapter 9: Photography and Videography   125

Hate to have picture taken ❦ photographer/videographer unavailable ❦ found cheaper photographer ❦ camera malfunctioned ❦ missing photographs.

Chapter 10: The Caterer and Reception   141

Reception site not available ❦ caterer overbooked ❦ no alcohol allowed ❦ can't use candles or Sterno ❦ fire at reception ❦ caterer served meat to vegetarians ❦ inebriated guests ❦ reception site too small ❦ wedding cake collapsed ❦ want to avoid bouquet and garter toss.

Chapter 11: Invitations and Gifts   163

Stationer went out of business ❦ invitations not ready on time ❦ programs are missing ❦ need more envelopes ❦ invitations on wrong paper stock ❦ calligrapher messed up ❦ invitations include errors ❦ guests not RSVPing ❦ problems with gift registry ❦ thank-you notes ❦ need more postage.

Chapter 12: Flowers, Rings, and Transportation   183

Florist not available ❦ florist ordered wrong flowers ❦ bride is allergic to flowers ❦ bees swarming on flowers ❦ rings not ready in time ❦ limo was dirty ❦ limo was MIA.

Chapter 13: The Honeymoon   199

Travel agency closed up shop ❦ honeymoon plans gone awry ❦ airline stopped flying ❦ lost tickets ❦ missed flight ❦ resort is overbooked ❦ resort is a dump ❦ cruise ship is contaminated ❦ illness on honeymoon ❦ hurricane hit ❦ destination is politically unstable.

Appendix   215

How to find vendors that won't make you feel anxious, plus questions to ask of them and what to put in your contract with them.

Index   219

About the Author   223

Introduction

As a well-published author and recognized expert on weddings, I've interviewed, spoken with, and given advice to hundreds of brides-to-be. This advice has come in many forms: my work as a wedding book author (*The Balanced Bride, The Portable Wedding Consultant*); as a writer and editor for bridal magazines (*Modern Bride, Bridal Guide, For the Bride, Elegant Wedding*); and as a spokesperson for national companies such as Sears and Hewlett-Packard. Despite the topics I may be tackling for the wedding markets, what worries the majority of brides-to-be and most often what they want to talk candidly about are the worst-case scenarios and "what ifs" of weddings—that is, "What if my dress doesn't fit?" or "What if the band sounds terrible?" or "What if my reception hall burns down?"

Because we put such great importance on our wedding days—plus the sizeable price tag on today's modern weddings—it is understandable that brides-to-be worry about these potential disasters. And disasters do happen. Why else would the 300,000 members of the Independent Insurance Agents and Brokers of America offer wedding insurance policies to their clients? Because wedding disasters are a reality.

Do a Google search of wedding disasters and you'll likely come up with news reports ranging from the limo driver who attempted to extort more money from the bride and groom at the last minute (*The New York Post*) to the reception hall that went bankrupt the week before three wedding receptions were to take place there (*The Philadelphia Inquirer*) to the bridal salon that flooded during spring rains, thus ruining thousands of dollars worth of wedding gowns (NBC's *Today* show).

Admittedly, most weddings go off without a major hitch, but small snafus can still happen as they do in everyday life, such as misplacing airline tickets or falling ill at the most inconvenient time. Someone once said not to sweat the small stuff, but that's exactly what brides-to-be do—and for good reason. Every woman has dreamed about having the perfect wedding since she was a little girl. Not surprisingly, this lifelong dream results in the bride-to-be putting a tremendous amount of pressure on herself to ensure that everything goes perfectly on her big day. And that's where this book comes in.

The idea behind *The Complete Guide for the Anxious Bride* is simple: to give you comfort by taking potential worst-case wedding scenarios and providing fabulous ways to either avoid or fix them. I don't want to add stress to an already-stressed woman. The idea here is that, heaven forbid, a bride finds herself facing a potential wedding-day fiasco, she'll be able to use the advice in *The Complete Guide for the Anxious Bride* to avert disaster or figure out a way to fix things before it's too late.

Chapter 1
Health Concerns

Q: I'm supposed to get my period on my wedding day. I don't want to deal with carrying around tampons and such.

A: Isn't it great to be a woman? Here, you've probably spent the past few months planning the most perfect day, and you happened to glance at your menstrual calendar (You *do* have a menstrual calendar, right?) and notice that the big P is due on the big W (wedding) day. So what can you do?

First, you can hope that the stress of your impending wedding will shift off your period a bit. It has happened before, and it could happen to you. However, if you don't want to leave your period to chance, here are some other options to consider.

Are you currently using a hormone-based birth control method? If so, you may be able to extend your monthly dose to "trick" your body into not menstruating. Mary Jane Lewitt, a certified nurse midwife in Atlanta, Georgia, and a member of the American College of Nurse Midwives explains:

"First, always check with your healthcare provider before extending your use of hormones to avoid menstruating. Some doctors will consult with patients over the phone, which means you don't need to schedule an appointment, but do check with him or her first.

"Second, if you're already taking birth control pills, double-check with your doctor about what kind of pill you're taking. Because there is more than one kind of birth control pills on the market these days, what kind of pill you take may affect your ability to put off your period.

"There are what's called 'monophasic' birth control pills, meaning that all the pills are identical in the levels of hormone they contain. That is, of the three weeks that you're taking pills, all of the pills are the same. The fourth week is the placebo week, and those pills do not include any hormones. Your body begins menstruating when there's a drop in hormones, so your period starts on the placebo week—when your body's not getting the same level of hormones anymore. If you skip the fourth or placebo week and start taking a new pack of pills immediately, you won't get your period. (FYI, some of the brand names of monophasic pills include—but are not limited to—Ortho-Novum, Ortho-Cyclene, Mercet, Yasmin, and Demulen.)

"There are two monophasic pills that you have to be careful about, because they are progesterone-only pills. (Most other pills contain both estrogen and progesterone.) They go by the names of Nor-QD and Micronor, so if you're taking them, be sure to discuss things with your healthcare practitioner carefully before continuing your pill-taking without a break for menstruation.

"Then there are what's called 'triphasic' birth control pills. These differ from monophasic pills because the dose of hormones changes each week that you're on the pill. During the first week of taking triphasic pills, the dose of hormone is pretty low. The second week the dose is a little higher, and the third week it's the highest. You can do the same on triphasic pills as you would on monophasic pills, tricking your body into not menstruating by starting back on Week One of the pills. However, because the hormone level is automatically lower in that first week's dose, you could have spotting or breakthrough bleeding. (Brand names of some triphasic pills include—but are not limited to—Ortho Tri-Cyclene, Tri-Norinyl, and Estrostep.)

"Birth control pills aren't the only hormone-based contraception these days. There's also Depo-Provera, which women get in shot form and which usually causes all menstruation to cease anyway. (If you suffer from breakthrough bleeding while using Depo-Provera, though, you can speak with your healthcare provider about getting additional hormones in pill or patch form to make your period stop completely for your wedding week. Or you can simply get your Depo-Provera shot a week earlier than usual.)

"Speaking of the patch, this is one of the newer birth control methods that use hormones. Women put the patch on every week for three weeks straight, then take it off for the fourth week to induce menstruation. If you just apply the patch again on Week Four and continue wearing it, you won't get your period. (The patch works identically to the monophasic pill—it just uses a different delivery method.) However, because the patch is still such a new method on the market, its 'off-label use' of period skipping is still being studied for safety and efficacy so your healthcare provider may suggest using a different method for skipping your period.

"Another new hormone-based contraception is the vaginal ring. You insert one ring and keep it in place continuously for three weeks, then take it out and throw it away. Once the hormones are out of your system, you get your period. Instead of waiting a week and getting your period, you can put a new ring in immediately. (Like the patch, the hormone levels in the ring are identical to monophasic pills.)"

According to Lewitt, this use of hormonal contraception to stop menstruation is done fairly commonly to treat medical problems, such as migraines during the menstrual cycle or women who suffer from heavy bleeding. "We don't recommend going for more than three months without having your cycle," she stresses.

If you're not currently taking the pill, have no medical conditions that would prevent you from doing so, and you still have a couple of months before the big day, discuss the option of starting the pill or another hormone-based contraception when you see your doctor. Just make sure you give yourself enough time between starting this form of contraception and your wedding day, because it may take a cycle or two for your hormones to get fully regulated.

Finally, if fooling Mother Nature by extending your use of hormone-based contraception won't work for you for whatever reason, just make sure that you're prepared. That is, wherever you'll be staying the night before your wedding or getting dressed the day of your wedding, plan for that place to be fully stocked with tampons, pads, pain relievers, and anything else you need to deal with and feel better once your period starts. The same thing goes for whatever handbag, purse, or satchel you'll be carrying—or your maid of honor will be carrying for you. Along with lipstick, pressed powder, and other essentials you'll need on hand for touch-ups, toss in some sanitary products as well.

Better yet, if you think that your period might start after the festivities have begun, put a just-in-case panty liner in your undergarments so that should you begin to bleed, you won't have to worry about an unsightly stain on your dress.

Q: I just got my period this morning! Now I'm bloated, have major cramps, and I'm getting married in a few hours.

A: Got bridesmaids? Get them to a drugstore. Just because you weren't prepared with tampons, pain relievers, and other accoutrements that go along with getting your period that's no reason for you to feel miserable on your big day. Unless you're getting married in the middle of nowhere, chances are someone in your wedding party or family can run to the nearest pharmacy and get you medicine to feel better, and sanitary products to prevent stains (or someone will have some with them). Don't be a martyr today—take some pain relievers (especially those that supposedly help to reduce bloating if that's what you normally take), drink a little something that might settle your stomach (such as regular cola), and, if you can, try to get a little exercise. Did you know that breaking a sweat actually helps to reduce the nasty side effects of your period? Take a 20-minute walk to feel better, and I'm confident that you will.

Q: I got my period last night at the rehearsal dinner. What am I supposed to do with tampons on my wedding day?

A: As previously mentioned, this is one of those situations where it's great to have bridesmaids. Not that you want to stick them with the job of schlepping around sanitary products, but if you have to, I'm sure they'll be happy to help. Are you going to be carrying a purse on the day of your wedding? Along with lipstick, pressed powder, and other essentials you'll need on hand for touch-ups, bring along some sanitary products as well. Similarly, you're likely not going to be the only menstruating woman at your wedding and reception, so why not ask one of your maids to run to the drugstore and buy a few boxes of sanitary products to stock in the bathrooms? That way you'll make the lives of your guests easier should their periods sneak up on them as well. Also, you'll have a surefire place to duck when you need a tampon or sanitary pad.

You (or your maids) may want to plan ahead and create an "essentials basket" for the bathroom at the reception location. These baskets can contain everything from tampons and sanitary napkins, hairspray, extra panty hose, and inexpensive combs to pain relievers, antacids, clear nail polish (for runs in your or a guest's stockings), breath freshener, travel sewing kits, safety pins, spare earring backs, spray deodorant, lotions, nail glue, and even baby wipes (which have been known to help with minor wine stains)! This idea can be slightly tailored for the men's restrooms as well by excluding the feminine products, nail glue and polish and substituting such things as men's styling products, inexpensive cologne, condoms, and disposable razors.

Q: My fiancé and I couldn't wait any longer and we had sex the night after my bridal shower. Now it's our wedding day, and I'm nauseous. Am I just nervous or could this be morning sickness?

A: It could be nerves or it could be a pregnancy. First things first, did you use protection? While no birth control method is 100-percent guaranteed, if you are on the pill (and taking it religiously) or you used condoms, it does decrease your likelihood of being pregnant—but not completely. So why not give yourself some peace of mind and take a pregnancy test? There are plenty of store-bought tests that can predict a pregnancy with great accuracy—even if you're just a few weeks pregnant or can't use first-thing-in-the-morning urine as the directions are likely to suggest. So run out to the drugstore (or send a close friend or relative out for you) and get a pregnancy test. No drugstore around? Or it's closed now and won't open in time before your wedding? Well then, play it safe. Avoid alcohol at the wedding reception (you can just touch your lips to a champagne glass during a toast and make it look like you're drinking it) until you know for sure.

If it turns out that you are pregnant, well, then congratulations! Yes, everyone is going to eventually do the math and figure out that you walked down the aisle with child, but think about it this way: You're married, and there's no better time to start a family than when you're legally husband and wife. Sure, having a baby so soon in your marriage may mess up some of your long-term plans, such as traveling or going to graduate school, but truth be told, there's never a perfect time to have a baby. So make the best of your pregnancy and your impending parenthood.

Q: We've both got laryngitis, and it looks like we're going to have to croak our vows. What should we do?

A: When it comes to illness and the wedding day, I think the best course of medicine is this: Call your doctor. If you can, get in to see him or her. If not, have a phone consultation to determine whether what you have is contagious or not. If you are contagious, you may want to seriously consider postponing your celebration. You're going to be meeting and greeting hundreds of people that day, and the last thing you want to do is send your guests away from your wedding with a virus. Have your doctor determine whether your laryngitis is from too much screaming at last night's concert or a bona fide bug. If it's the latter, you've got a tough call to make, but postponing your wedding and celebration may be in everyone's best interest. Think about it this way—if you're sick on your wedding day, you're likely going to be sick on your honeymoon. How much of a bummer would it be to be so under the weather that not only can't you enjoy your happy day, but also you can't enjoy the vacation that follows?

Also, I would advise that any couple tying the knot during flu season—generally, late fall and all of winter—get a flu shot before the season begins. You may want to advise your wedding party members and parents to do the same. That way you lessen the chances of the people in your wedding coming down with the flu on or before your wedding day.

It's situations such as this that confirm my belief in wedding insurance. I know that to the bride and the groom insuring your wedding day seems like a scam. But people have been insuring their vacations for years—including honeymoons. Why not spend a couple hundred bucks to give yourself peace of mind that, should something happen that makes canceling the wedding a reality, you're not out big bucks. That way if you do become too ill to walk down the aisle and you have to cancel your wedding, you'll be covered financially.

Q: I broke my leg and now I can't walk down the aisle.

A: True, a bride with a broken leg may not be able to walk down the aisle, but who says you can't hobble or, better yet, roll down the aisle? Sure, no one wants to look back on wedding pictures of a woman in a white gown and a wheelchair. But if all that's keeping you from going forward with your wedding is a cast and a little vanity, get over it. Think about the brevity you'll bring to your wedding by rolling down the aisle or gliding across the dance floor at your reception in your shiny new wheelchair? If you can find it within yourself to make the best of this situation, your wedding day will still turn out to be a great day. Of course, if your dream day includes schussing down the slopes to your waiting groom, then, yes, you'll probably have to rethink your wedding plans.

Q: My fiancé broke his arm just days before the wedding and his tuxedo won't fit around his cast.

A: Sounds like the groom has got to go jacketless. Plain and simple. Okay, so he may look a bit out of place in the wedding pictures because most grooms wear a jacket, but like the bride with the broken leg, you shouldn't let a little vanity or fear of being arrested by the fashion police make you cancel your wedding. Now, if you were planning to go scuba diving on your honeymoon, the cast will probably cause a problem. Therefore you should rethink your honeymoon plans or postpone the scuba diving trip for when your future husband has full use of both of his arms.

Q: Everyone came down with a stomach bug. It's the morning of the wedding and we're all throwing up instead of getting ready.

A: The one good thing about most stomach bugs is that they come and go within 24 hours. With this in mind, here's what I think you should do: Postpone the ceremony and reception but only for the short term. (Note to anxious brides: Here is yet another scenario where wedding insurance makes sense.) There's no reason to go through with things if you will be tossing cookies while your guests are tossing rice. Enlist your mother, your sister, and any close friends or relatives who did not get the bug into calling all the guests to let them know of the change of plans. If calling everyone isn't possible, you could always post a sign at the ceremony site letting people know that the wedding has been delayed due to illness.

If you were planning to tie the knot Saturday morning, why not see if your officiant, caterer, and others are available Sunday morning? If you happened to have planned your wedding in an off-season when weddings aren't at their peak, you may have luck with simply moving your wedding to 24 hours later.

If that doesn't work, say, for the caterer and musicians but does work for the officiant, you can throw together an ad hoc, last-minute wedding celebration at the home of somebody who lives nearby—if they offer, of course. Remember it will be casual and not at all what you expected. But you'll get the deed done—you'll be married—and you'll be able to celebrate with all the people whom you wanted to be there in the first place.

If the last-minute, postponed wedding doesn't work—and I'll admit that your chances of pulling it off may be quite slim—you'll definitely have to reschedule the wedding. You can choose to have the same kind of wedding and reception that you'd originally planned but at a later date, or you can choose to have an entirely different wedding, even one on a smaller scale or in a different locale. Just make sure that if you choose an option that prevents you from inviting all the original guests the second time around, you send a brief, handwritten note to each person who won't be receiving an invitation to explain why you had to change your plans and cut down your guest list. Maybe you lost money from the vendors whom you'd paid with cash only—and who wouldn't honor a refund. (Another note to anxious brides: This is a perfect reason to only use vendors that accept credit cards. If something goes wrong and you need a refund, when you pay for a service with a credit card, the credit card company will work on your behalf to make sure you're not charged for services not rendered.) Therefore, when it came time to plan the wedding celebration again, you simply had a smaller budget to work with. Or maybe you decided to plan a smaller wedding overall and simply don't have the room to invite everyone. As long as you take the time to explain these new circumstances to friends and family, no one should be offended.

Q: My father got sick and now he can't walk me down the aisle.

A: First, I hope your father is feeling better very soon. I know that it is mostly every woman's dream to have her daddy walk her down the aisle on her big day, but sometimes fate intervenes and that's not possible. While it may seem catastrophic not to have your father on your arm, plenty of brides before you have made it to the altar solo—or with another person besides their father. Do you have an older brother who could step in? What about your mother? Are you okay with the notion of going it alone? Consider these options and see which one feels right for you.

If your father can't be at your wedding because of his injuries, see if your officiant, house of worship or ceremony location can arrange some sort of wireless hook up—be it a digital camcorder or phone of some sort. That way your ceremony can be broadcast to wherever it is your father will be resting and recuperating. Just because your father can't be there in person to walk you down the aisle doesn't mean that he can't be there to participate in the ceremony, albeit electronically. If technology will allow, your father may even be able to "give you away" via modem or whatever hook-up you can work out. So he may not be there in person, but he'll definitely be there in spirit.

Now let's say your father is well enough to attend but not strong enough to walk you down the aisle. Can you wheel him down the aisle in a wheelchair? Could you have your father seated in a position of honor at the altar? That way you'll walk down by yourself and you can meet him at the front of the church or synagogue. Then, when he "gives you away," someone can guide him to his seat. Or you can have someone else walk you down the aisle (if you don't want to go it alone) in your father's place—your dad can sit in one of the front pews with your mom—and you can ask that your officiant to make an announcement either before or during the ceremony about how lucky we are to have the bride's father here with us today, even though illness prevents him from walking his daughter down the aisle, or something like that. Doing so will give your father a place of honor and make him feel special at your wedding, even if he can't walk you down the aisle.

> ### Wedding Wisdom
>
> We were forced to deal with my fiancé's father passing away three weeks prior to our wedding, which brought our world to a halt as we knew it. It was extremely tough, because the man who had talked about this wedding incessantly for a year would not be with us. We kept the wedding ceremony as planned and felt that he was there in spirit the day we got married.
> –Emily, Ohio

Q: One of our parents got sick and can't be at the wedding. Should we cancel?

A: The solution to your situation is similar to the one where the bride's father fell ill and couldn't walk her down the aisle. While a knee-jerk reaction may be to cancel, with today's technology there's no reason to. Your sick parent may not be able to participate in your wedding in person, but he or she can be there electronically if you'd like. Perhaps the only reason to cancel a wedding due to a sick parent is if that parent was literally hosting the wedding—at his or her home. Then it may not be fully appropriate to go on with the festivities without him or her around, and you may want to consider postponing. Again, it's situations like this that make wedding insurance such a no-brainer.

Q: My father broke his foot just days before the wedding. Now he can't walk me down the aisle.

A: Says who? Unless your father's doctor has instructed him to remain in bed, there's no reason why your dad still can't get you down the aisle. Just realize that your dad will likely hobble, rather than walk, or roll down the aisle (if he's in a wheelchair). As long as you're flexible about how your father participates, a broken foot shouldn't get in the way of a great wedding day.

Now as far as logistics are concerned, with your father on crutches, using a cane, or sitting in a wheelchair, your procession may take a bit longer than planned. Do discuss this possibility with whatever musician you're using at the ceremony. They may have to be prepared to repeat your processional song accordingly, or you may have to choose a new and longer piece of music to allow for you and your father's longer-than-expected descent down the aisle.

Chapter 2
Beauty Emergencies

Q: I woke up this morning with a monster stress zit in the middle of my forehead. Help!

A: First and foremost, do not pick at the pimple. "It is hard to resist the temptation, but the bride should not pinch or squeeze lesions," warns Asra Ali, M.D., assistant professor of dermatology at the University of Texas Medical School at Houston. "If the pimple and skin are handled too often, infected material may go deeper into the skin and this could cause additional inflammation and possible scarring or dark blotches. When you expose the contents of a pimple to surrounding skin, you can increase inflammation and redness."

However, if the pimple looks as though it's about to erupt, Audrey Kunin, M.D., a Kansas City-based dermatologist, and founder and president of Dermadoctor.com, says it's okay to relieve some of the pressure inside the pimple by giving it a gentle squeeze. (Try holding a tissue between your fingers for a more gentle touch.) It may make the pimple look a little better, but you also risk making it look a lot worse as well.

If you discover this monster zit in the days before your wedding, get thee to a dermatologist! The doctor will likely inject the pimple with a steroid solution to calm the redness and inflammation, says Dr. Ali, who believes if you call a dermatologist and explain your pre-wedding pimple situation, "I am sure the bride could be accommodated."

Let's say time or distance won't allow for a dermatologist's visit. Here are some other solutions to try:

- Apply a topical benzyl peroxide gel to try to dry up the pimple a bit.
- Apply a topical steroid to reduce swelling. (Dr. Ali warns that you should use an over-the-counter steroid cream for only a day or so.) Dr. Kunin recommends looking for a product that is one-percent cortisone.
- "Take Tylenol or Motrin (if you know they are safe for you to take)," says Dr. Kunin, "as these systemic anti-inflammatory medications can also help reduce inflammation on your skin."

Finally, if you can't get to a pharmacy or doctor and find yourself on the morning of your wedding dealing with a pimple, look no further than your toiletries bag for a quick fix—you'll find it in your tube of toothpaste.

"There is no question that the use of toothpaste to zap a zit fast is one of those time-honored home remedies," says Dr. Kunin. "As the toothpaste dries, it helps to dehydrate the pimple and to absorb the sebum (oil) from the affected sebaceous gland much like a clay masque functions." Dr. Kunin says the toothpastes that work best as a pimple treatment are those that are white, are in cream form (not a gel), do not contain whitening ingredients (which can burn the skin), and aren't cinnamon flavored (since cinnamon is a known skin irritant).

Q: How can I avoid looking oily or shiny in all of my pictures?
A: You will become one with pressed powder on your wedding day, lest you be deemed the happy, shiny bride. You see, pressed powder (not diamonds) is a girl's best friend for blotting oil and giving you a gorgeous matte complexion. So make sure you have a compact case of powder with you

at all times—or assign one of your attendants as your makeup watchdog so she can let you know when you need a touch-up of powder.

Also, your groom might need some pressed powder, too. I'll never forget on my wedding day when my photographer suggested we blot the shine on my husband's face, forehead and, dare I say, scalp, because he was shining like crazy. It may not seem very masculine for a man to use pressed powder, but trust me, your photographer will thank you—and your pictures will look great—if you and your groom keep the shine to a minimum with regular touch-ups throughout the event.

Q: My dentist just recommended that I get braces right away. What am I going to do? I don't want to be a metal mouth in my wedding pictures.

A: Okay, so the bad news is you need to get braces. Want to hear the good news? These days you have plenty of options when it comes to orthodontia as an adult.

In addition to braces of different colors—maybe you'll go for white on white to match your wedding gown?—there are also braces made with clear plastic, those that are attached to the back of your teeth (so no one can see them), and braces that aren't braces at all but more like invisible mouth guard contraptions that do the job of braces. So be sure to discuss all your options with your orthodontist—including whether you can wait a few weeks until after your wedding to get braces—before making your final decision. Yes, braces will improve your smile and your bite, but you have to weigh that with how potentially miserable you'll be on your big day if you have to get braces beforehand.

Q: I ripped my contact lenses and don't have any extras. I don't want to wear my glasses at the wedding. Do I have any other choices?

A: You know what's great about being the bride at the wedding? You don't have to read anything at the wedding or reception and can probably get away without wearing any corrective lenses at all. Reciting vows? Just repeat after the officiant. Reading a toast? It's the best man's job. Smiling for the camera? No need to see the photographer. See, it'll be a piece of wedding cake.

Now when it comes to greeting people in the receiving line, things could get a little dicey. When I don't wear my glasses, I may be as blind as a newborn kitten—especially when dealing with distances. But if you're in my face, I can usually see you. If your eyesight is like mine, you should be fine in your receiving line. If you need an extra set of eyes, ask your husband or maid of honor to pinch-hit for you. If he or she stands first in the receiving line and says everyone's name out loud as they approach, you'll know who's coming and how to address them, and it won't matter that all you may see are fuzzy shapes.

"Aunt Matilda, I'm so glad you could make it," is all that needs to be said for you to know that the next set of hands you'll shake or pair of lips that you feel planted on one of your cheeks will be Aunt Matilda. Similarly, as you mingle at the reception, keep your husband or maid of honor nearby so one of them can run interference with any approaching (and blurry) people who will expect a greeting.

Finally, you can have a sense of humor about your lost-contact situation and make an announcement at the reception. Tell everyone gathered that while you're happy to see them at your wedding, you can't actually "see" them because you ripped a contact, lost a contact, broke your glasses, or whatever happened to render your eyesight less than perfect. (One bride I know accidentally flushed her glasses down the toilet and turned that unfortunate event into the big day's big joke.) That way your guests will know that they'll have to announce themselves when they come up to speak to you, and I'm sure everyone will have a good sense of humor about the whole thing. Of course, keeping an extra set of contacts in your purse seems to be a good disaster plan, but thinking about this preventative measure after the fact doesn't help much, does it?

Q: I took off my glasses while taking pictures at the reception, and I think the busboy bussed them away. Now we can't find them and I can't see anything.

A: Just like the bride who lost or ripped her contact lenses, you've got to figure out an action plan fast for getting through the big day—even though you can't see anything. Here are your two options:

1. You can assign someone with excellent vision to be your extra set of eyes, such as your new husband, your maid of honor, or a bridesmaid. This person's job is to tell you ahead of time who is coming over to give you a kiss or wish you congratulations so you can address the person by name.
2. You can be up front with your gathered guests that your eyeglasses seem to have left on an early honeymoon—and left you unable to see anything beyond the tip of your nose. Once people know that your vision is less than perfect, I'm sure they'll help you out by telling you who they are when they speak with you.

Finally, like the person who risks losing her contacts, you, the eyeglasses wearer, should keep an extra pair of glasses on hand. You just never know when a pair might break or get lost—I always bring an extra pair of glasses with me when I travel—and doing so will be great insurance for your eyesight and your peace of mind.

Q: One of our attendants had emergency oral surgery a few days before the wedding and now has a swollen face.

A: So how does this attendant feel about his or her swollen face? Is he or she okay with or exceedingly embarrassed by his or her appearance? In a situation such as this, where someone in your wedding may look less than perfect in your eyes due to something health-related—whether it's emergency surgery or a broken limb—you, the bride, should always give that person the opportunity to back out of being in the wedding, especially if that person is uncomfortable with how the broken foot or swollen jaw has left him or her feeling and looking. However, you should not tell the person that he or she can't be in your wedding party anymore because of his or her outward appearance. That's just plain rude. Now should you give that person the option of going forward, you need to find peace with your swollen or injured attendant's decision, and try not to let yourself get too caught up in the fact that he or she may look a bit off, if you will, in your wedding photos. You can't control if someone gets injured or needs emergency surgery before your wedding, but you can control how you react to and deal with it.

Q: I decided to get a little tan before the wedding and used a tanning booth. Now I'm burned to a crisp! Is there anything I can do?

A: There are two things that you should do right away to help you feel better. One is to take some sort of medication that is also an anti-inflammatory, such as acetaminophen or ibuprofen. "Either of these drugs will help to reduce inflammation and control pain," says Asra Ali, M.D., an assistant professor of dermatology at the University of Texas Medical School at Houston.

The other is to drink plenty of liquids, such as water. Why? Being burned means you're likely to be dehydrated. You'll counteract dehydration by drinking liquids and replenishing your fluids.

Dr. Ali also recommends applying cool compresses to burned skin multiple times a day and avoiding additional sun exposure until the skin is feeling better. Audrey Kunin, M.D., a Kansas City-based dermatologist, creator of Dermadoctor specialist skin care, and founder and president of Dermadoctor.com, suggests that you dip the compresses in a cooled brew of green tea. "Green tea acts as an antioxidant and helps to reduce inflammation," she adds.

If these at-home remedies don't work, Dr. Ali suggests you call your doctor, who may prescribe a five-day course of prednisone, which will reduce swelling and, she adds, "work wonders to decrease the discomfort."

Finally, if you're set on looking tan on your big day, spring for a skin-bronzing treatment at a local salon instead of going for the real thing. That way you can have the little bit of color that you crave on your wedding day without doing any long-term damage to your skin. In addition, by paying a professional to do your skin bronzing, you'll be assured that you won't end up with orange-looking skin or any unsightly streaks. While most self-tanners have improved over the years, I think for your wedding you should go for the professional skin bronzing, just to be on the safe side.

A less expensive option than a salon skin bronzing might be going to a tanning center that offers a skin-bronzing booth. What this means is you strip down and step into a booth where they spray on a fake tan on you—instead of having your bake your skin in a tanning bed.

Q: My hairdresser left the salon where I always go and no one knows how to get in touch with her. Now there's no one to do my hair—and she was going to do my makeup, too!

A: While it's awfully unprofessional of your stylist to up and leave like that, it's not the end of the world. As with all vendors that you'll hire for your wedding, it's important to go with someone who comes highly recommended and whom you can trust. So, it's likely that some of your friends have a stylist/makeup artist to whom they can refer you. Start asking all of your female friends and colleagues (whose hair you admire) to whom they go for cuts, coloring, and styling. See if they like their stylist enough to hire him/her to do their hair at their weddings or for a special event. If they give the stylist the thumbs-up, then start visiting the salons of these recommended stylist. If you can, get at least one haircut or color job (if you color your hair) with this stylist and a practice makeup application so you'll have firsthand experience on which to base your decision, and then go from there. You may find the perfect stylist on your first call or visit, or it may take five or six. Hopefully, you'll find the perfect person for the job. If you don't, you can always reassess your expectations for how your hair and makeup will look and simply do them yourself. However, given how crazed you'll likely be on the big day, I wouldn't advise this do-it-yourself option.

Wedding Wisdom

If I were to give one piece of advice to a bride-to-be, it would be to have someone come to her place to do her hair and makeup the day of the wedding. I got one hour of sleep the night before my wedding, and it was wonderful to just sit and drink coffee while my makeup artist transformed me into a beautiful bride!
–Diane, Virginia

Q: I called my hairdresser to ask him a question and discovered that he forgot to book my date. Now he's not available to do my hair.

A: Hey, mistakes happen and if this is the first time that your hairdresser forgot you, then let him off the hook and figure out a Plan B. If this is indicative of his attitude, then you may need to find yourself a new stylist—permanently. Regardless of whom you hire in the future to do your hair on a regular basis, here's what you should do for your wedding-day dilemma.

Does your stylist work in a well-staffed salon? Has anyone else there ever done your hair? At the salon I use, there have been times when my regular stylist was overbooked and I had to make an appointment with another stylist there. While I wasn't happy at first about trying somebody new—funny how we women become territorial about who works on our hair—I'm glad that I did. Now I know that in a pinch, there are at least two other stylists at my salon ith whom I feel very comfortable. I hope you've had a similar, positive experience at your salon and can book an alternate hairstylist from the salon.

If not, then it's time to poll your friends, families, and work colleagues with great hair (Ask only those with great hair, please. You do't want to hire the stylist that made your friend look like a clown), and ask them if they would recommend their own stylist for special-occasion hair. In a situation such as this, it's best to go with a stylist that someone you know and respect (and whose hair you love) recommends. The last thing you want to be doing in the days, weeks and months before your wedding is trying out a new stylist or colorist. This is not the time to experiment. By asking around you'll be sure to find the perfect stand-in stylist—and he or she may be someone you like so much that you start using regularly.

Q: My hairstylist double-booked me, and now she's sending a stylist I've never met. My stylist was supposed to do my makeup, too. I don't want a stranger doing my hair and makeup on my wedding day.

A: Unless you're willing to do your hair and makeup yourself, it looks like you're going to have to let a stranger do them both on your wedding day. That said, be sure you hire a person who comes highly recommended from someone you know—and whom you think has great hair. Don't meet her for the first time on your wedding day. Make sure that you schedule a trial run with this person so you can feel confident that your vision of an updo and the new stylist's vision of an updo mesh, and that she does makeup just the way you like it.

Q: My hairstylist just announced that she's raised her prices. Now I can't afford to use her for my wedding.

A: Do you know for a fact that she's going to charge you more for doing your wedding-day hair? Have you asked her about this or are you just assuming that she's going to charge more than you originally thought? Do you have something in writing from her, confirming her original prices? If so, she should really honor your original agreement, and you should discuss this issue with her immediately. If you never confirmed her fees before they went up, still see if she will negotiate with you. In my experience most stylists want to keep long-time clients happy and will often make concessions in order to do so. It could be that the price increase was a salon mandate—and therefore not the stylist's decision. In this case see if your stylist will "freelance" for your wedding and come to your home or meet you at a third-party location (such as the ceremony site) so she can charge you a fee that you both agree upon, and not one that her boss back at the salon is telling her she needs to charge. If none of these scenarios work, you can always just pay the higher fee—and adjust your wedding budget accordingly—or find a new stylist.

Q: My friend's hairdresser is way cheaper than mine and even though I've already booked my hairdresser, I'm tempted to go with someone cheaper. Can I do that?

A: Before you think about this decision in terms of straight dollars and sense, think about this: How do you feel about your friend's hair? Are you always complimenting her whenever she comes back from getting it done? Or is your friend always apologizing for the fact that her stylist goofed yet again in figuring out exactly what she wanted done to her hair? Is your friend's favorite phrase, "You can always grow out a bad cut?"

If it's the former—and the cost savings is significant and you won't damage your relationship with your current stylist—then sure, investigate that possibility. But don't cancel with your original stylist until after you know for sure that your friend's stylist is available and you like him or her.

However, if the latter best describes your friend's hair situation, I'd say stick with what you got, regardless of price, and know that you'll have peace of mind about how your hair looks on your big day.

Q: I never do my hair or wear makeup, but everyone tells me that I have to get them both done for the wedding. I don't want to end up looking like some overdone doll.

A: Just because you get your hair done on your wedding day doesn't mean you're going to end up looking like a doll or a beauty pageant contestant. The biggest reason to hire someone to do your hair (and your makeup) is so you have one less thing to worry about on what's sure to be a stressful and busy day. If you know that a stylist will be at your house at 10 a.m. and the makeup person is coming at 11 a.m., then you needn't run around that morning trying to make sure your hair looks perfect or that your mascara doesn't leave you looking like a raccoon.

Believe me, I'm not saying this because I'm getting kickbacks from the beauty industry (which I'm not). I'm like you—I'm lucky if I remember to brush my hair most days of the week, although when I have the time, I enjoy styling my hair. However, doing my hair up fancy is not one of my day-to-day priorities, so I don't make time for it. However, there are times when looking my best means a lot to me, and then I always turn to a professional.

Besides writing books, I appear on TV frequently, and while I'm about as far from a prima donna as they come, the one thing that I always request whenever possible is to have a hair and makeup person at the TV studio. I figure that if I can leave the worrying about how I look to someone else, I can use all of my energy to focus on doing a good job on TV.

You should use the same logic when it comes to your wedding. Why should you have to worry about getting your hair or makeup just so, when what you should be spending your mental energy on is preparing for your walk down the aisle? Wouldn't it be nice to know that there will be someone there the morning of to take the shine off your forehead and nose, and to make your hair super shiny? Remember: There are going to be lots of people taking pictures of you on your wedding day, and if you don't wear any makeup or do anything to your hair, you may not be happy with how you look in your photos. Just think about exactly how you want to remember yourself looking on your big day. If, in the end, going au naturel with your hair and makeup is no big deal to you, then don't worry about hiring a makeup artist or stylist. However, if you wouldn't mind a little extra help in the hair and makeup department, speak with your friends about people they've used in a similar capacity for special occasion hair and makeup, and hire the person or persons you like the best, feel most comfortable with, and who fits your budget.

Q: My maid of honor convinced me to get acrylic nails done. Now they're super long, and I'm afraid I won't be able to eat or shake hands with people at the wedding.

A: I applaud you for indulging in something such as getting acrylic nails done before your wedding. I think it's very important to have your hands looking lovely on your big day—especially because so many people are going to be looking at the new wedding ring on your hand. That's why I think a pre-wedding manicure is always a good idea.

That said, give yourself a few days to get used to having these new nails. Granted you probably won't be the most proficient typist with longer-than-usual nails, but by the time your wedding rolls around, your new nails should feel perfectly normal and you'll be shaking hands and holding forks just fine. If, though, after you've had them for a few days you really hate them, go back to the salon and have them taken off. There's no reason to be uncomfortable or feeling self-conscious about your nails on your big day.

Q: My father wears a toupee and my fiancé's father has the stupidest comb-over I've ever seen. I think they'll both look ridiculous in my wedding photographs, and I want them to fix their hair before the big day.

A: How would you feel if your fiancé suddenly turned to you and said, "Hey, honey, I know that you love being a brunette, but I've decided that I want a blonde bride. How about dying your hair for our wedding?" That would seem pretty ballsy of him to make such a suggestion, right? I mean, shouldn't you be the one who makes the decision about how you look or what color hair you choose to wear? Well, you should apply the same courtesy to your father and your future father-in-law. I'm sure that they're already self-conscious enough about being "follically challenged," which is why they're trying to cover up their lack of hair with a toupee and a comb-over. Please don't bring this issue up with them. Instead try to look beyond their less-than-perfect hairstyles for the people you care about and want to be there to celebrate with you at your wedding. So what if their hair looks ridiculous to you in your photographs? That's your problem, not theirs. After all, pictures are meant to capture important moments and what we look like at those moments, not what we wish we looked like.

Chapter 3
Sticky Situations

Q: I've heard of wedding vendors ripping off brides by asking for cash up front—then skipping town. Now some of my vendors are telling me that they want cash only, and I don't want them to rip me off.

A: Here's one really big reason why you never want to pay cash for anything related to your wedding day—if you do and a vendor doesn't come through for you, you're out that money and there's nothing you can do about it. However, if you pay for everything with a credit card, you've got the credit card company to back you up if you decide to dispute the charge, and you've got the law on your side.

Since 1974, the Fair Credit Billing Act has protected consumers against unauthorized credit card charges or, in the case of a couple hiring vendors for a wedding, "charges for goods and services [that] weren't delivered as agreed," according to the Federal Trade Commission (FTC) Website at *www.ftc.gov*. (The FTC enforces the Fair Credit Billing Act.) What that means is if a vendor promises to cater, photograph, or play music at your wedding; deliver your wedding gown; or any other situation where you could likely pay for services with a credit card—and then doesn't do as promised—you can report that violation to the FTC and use the criteria of the Fair Credit Billing Act to sue the unreliable vendor. (You can get the details on how to file a violation on the FTC Website.)

There are a few caveats involving the Fair Credit Billing Act. The first is the dispute must be for more than $50. Second, the charge in question must have occurred in your home state or within 100 miles of your current billing address. (That means that if you're planning a long-distance wedding, you may not be as successful in disputing charges.) And third, you must have made a good faith effort first to settle the dispute before bringing in the big guns, such as a lawsuit. (In this instance you're likely to be able to prove a good faith effort that failed by keeping copies of all correspondence and sending it by certified mail. However, be sure to consult a legal expert if a situation like this arises so you'll feel confident that you've satisfied the notion of a good faith effort.)

Legal mumbo jumbo aside, I'm sure there are plenty of respectable wedding vendors out there, and chances are the ones you're dealing with are honest and upstanding. However, you simply can't take a chance. Explain to each of the cash-only vendors that you're uncomfortable paying in a way that offers you no protection or recourse, and that unless they will take a credit card, you'll have to take your business elsewhere. If they don't comply, accept that for your own protection you'll need to find someone else who takes credit cards to cater, photograph your wedding, or whatever service you need.

In today's world of small business owners and entrepreneurs, asking about taking credit cards isn't that unreasonable—and should be a no-brainer for these businesspeople. Don't feel bad about making this request.

Q: One of my vendors called to say that my deposit check bounced and now he doesn't want to do business with me.

A: I think you need to clarify things with this vendor and find out if a) he doesn't want to do business with you if you want to pay by check only or b) he doesn't want to do business with you at all. I can understand a business owner getting a bad taste in his mouth from a customer who bounced a check. And perhaps if you agree to pay for everything else with a credit card, he'll change his mind. Or maybe this vendor is so temperamental that it was a blessing in disguise that your check bounced. By getting to see his "real" side (as opposed to him on his best behavior because he wanted your business), you'll probably have saved yourself a lot of heartache if you find another, less moody vendor for your wedding instead of this guy.

Q: I know everyone told us to stick to our wedding budget, but we went a little crazy and now we're out of money. Is there a bank for brides and grooms to ring up for a loan?

A: Every story I've ever written for a magazine on wedding budgets shows one thing to be true—when it's all said and done, most couples end up spending 10 to 20 percent more than what they'd originally bargained for on their wedding. I hope every couple has similar wiggle room in their budget to cover some additional expenses, and if they don't, they should make arrangements to ensure that they do.

Because it sounds like you didn't plan for this, getting a loan may not be such a bad idea. In fact, the following financial tips would be appropriate for any couple feeling a pre-wedding pinch, whether your budget is running tight, one of you lost your job and simply won't have the income that you expected, or one of your parents originally promised to help pay for the wedding but can't now. Here are some ideas to consider.

Are interest rates amendable for a loan, such as a home equity loan, to cover your expenses? Does one of your employers offer any sort of tax-deferred deduction from your paycheck that will help you sock away the money you need in a short period of time? Is the bank of mom and dad available for assistance?

If you exhaust all of your financial resources and you still come up short, then you're going to have to cut some of the fat from your wedding budget. Perhaps you'd planned to have flowers on the aisle of each pew at the church. Forgoing flowers for simple bows could save you big bucks. Or maybe you were hoping to have an elaborate dessert table at your reception. Why not just cut and serve your wedding cake? Most guests are stuffed by the time the dessert course rolls around, so keep things simple (and inexpensive) by having your wedding cake be your only dessert. Look for things that you can modify in your budget, such as a deejay instead of a 12-piece orchestra, and you should have no problem making up the difference in your budget.

> ### *Wedding Wisdom*
>
> *We were married September 15, 2001....the weekend after September 11th. We live in Austin, and were married in Chicago, where we grew up and went to college. Because we wanted our chocolate lab, Bailey, to be in our wedding, we decided to drive from Texas to Chicago. For months, our mothers tried to talk us out of it, but we hit the road on Monday, September 10th. That first day we drove as far as Springfield, Missouri, spent the night, and started the drive to Chicago the next day at 8:30 a.m. We turned on the radio, and listened to the events of September 11th unfolding as we drove from Springfield to Chicago. We both knew that if it hadn't been for our stubbornness with having the dog at our wedding, we would be stuck in Austin, because all planes were grounded. On the day of our wedding, we didn't get our programs or flowers, and bridesmaids, groomsmen and best friends had no way to get to Chicago. But our families were there, and we were able to get married as planned, and that's all that mattered.*
> *–Katy, Texas*

Q: My grandmother is quite old and I'm afraid she might fall ill at my wedding.

A: If someone should become ill at your wedding, you must remember that these are the sorts of things that cannot be avoided, and it's not your fault. Although it is difficult dealing with an infirmed guest, you shouldn't let the situation ruin your event.

That said, the best way to handle a health emergency like this is to try to keep it as quiet as possible. You don't want to draw any additional attention to the sick guest, who may be feeling quite embarrassed about the fact that she may be causing a scene at your wedding. If your guest is well enough to walk, bring that person to another room where he or she can rest for the remainder of the night—or until that person is feeling well enough to return to the celebration. If things seem serious, err on the side of caution and have someone dial 911. Sure, having an ambulance pull up to your wedding will likely cause a commotion, but it will ensure that the sick guest will get necessary attention—and fast.

Q: I'm afraid my fiancé is going to drink too much at his bachelor party and will be hungover at the wedding.

A: Ask yourself this—is your fiancé known to be a big drinker or are you just worrying yourself about a hypothetical "what if"? If it's the latter, please don't pile more on your worry plate than you need to. Yes, men tend to drink at bachelor parties—and women at bachelorette parties—but that doesn't mean that your fiancé is going to get so smashed that he won't be able to walk down the aisle with you the next day. If one of the things that attracted you to your fiancé is the fact that he's a teetotaler (one who abstains from drinking any alcohol), then you probably don't have anything to worry about. If he doesn't usually drink much on a night out with the guys, I doubt he will at his bachelor party.

And speaking of the bachelor party, who says that it has to be the night before the wedding anyway? I understand that, traditionally, the men in the wedding party go out for a night on the town after being together with everyone at the rehearsal dinner. But if you know that your future husband is going to want to, shall we say, indulge and imbibe at his bachelor party, why not ask him (or his best man) to schedule it for a night other than the night before your wedding? That way he can go out and have fun, and you don't have to worry that he'll come back so stinking drunk that he'll need to cradle a bucket on the big day.

> ### Wedding Wisdom
>
> I was a lucky bride. Not only did I have a fiancé who was willing to spend the rest of his life with me, I had four loving parents who wanted to help make this the most special day of our lives. While this is a blessing, when it came to the down and dirty details, four parents caused a bit of stress. In the Jewish faith, both the mother and father walk the bride down the aisle. As the child of divorced and remarried parents, I was torn between bestowing this honor on my birth mother and father, and my stepfather, who played a major role in my upbringing. Of course, all four wanted to be part of the process. I ran the idea of having my father and stepmother start me off at the entrance and partway down the aisle, and hand me to my mother and stepfather for the last half of the trip. While this made sense in theory, both sets of parents wanted to be the "last" to say good-bye to me. Through a series of tactics, they attempted to persuade me in their individual approaches. In the end, I decided that all four would walk me in, my father and stepmother on my left, and my mother and stepfather on my right, but when we got to the last part of the aisle, I would walk the rest of the way on my own. My parents kissed me good-bye, and walked around the outsides of the aisles to take their seats up front. This solution avoided the appearance of picking "favorites" among my parents, and symbolized my independence in making this next important step in my life.
> —Amy, Massachusetts

Q: Some of my friends told me that they'd joked about my sordid dating past on camera with the videographer. I'm mortified because there's some stuff I've never revealed to my new husband.

A: You know how they always say that the best defense is a good offense? Well, that's what you need to do now. You've got to open up to your fiancé and share with him things about your past that you may have been hiding or didn't feel comfortable sharing with him. What makes a marriage or any relationship strong is honesty and open communication, and if you can't feel comfortable doing that with the guy you're going to marry, then you're likely to run into issues down the line when you have to deal with sensitive matters.

No one should go into a marriage without having a full and clear sense of who the person they're marrying really is. Also, by opening up and letting him know about some of the stuff that happened in the past, you can use that conversation to let him know, yet again, that you're completely confident in your decision to be with him for the rest of your life and can't wait to marry him.

So have that heart-to-heart with your husband-to-be as soon as you can. That way, if your friends get a little tipsy at the wedding reception and spill the beans on your secret crush from college, you won't have to worry that this news will come as a surprise to your fiancé. He'll already know the whole story.

Q: Just because my mother and father are paying for my wedding, they think they can call all of the shots. Should I call the whole thing off and just elope to prove my point?

A: Please don't go eloping just to spite your parents. It sounds like what you need is a good old-fashioned dose of improved communication. It's understandable for the parents who are picking up the wedding tab to feel that they have the right to make all of the decisions because it's their dough that's covering it all. But I always advise brides and grooms to be up front with their parents about what they, the engaged couple, expect with the wedding.

Schedule a time when you and your fiancé can sit down face-to-face with your parents or his if they're paying for the wedding. (If distance prevents that face-to-face meeting from happening, then schedule a time when you can all talk together on the phone.) Start off your conversation by thanking the parents for paying for the wedding, and let them know how appreciative you are of their generosity. Then say something such as,

"We have a couple of things we want to talk with you about, and we would really appreciate it if you could just listen to what we have to say."

Once you've got their attention, say "I know that you're really excited for us and want us to have the perfect wedding. But for us to have that perfect wedding, we really need to be the ones making the decisions." Explain that you'd like the parents to be involved in the decision-making process and that you respect their opinion. Promise that you'll run all the options by the parents beforehand, but make it clear that while you'll consider their input, you will be the ones who eventually decide which vendor you'll hire or which reception site you'll choose. Sometimes it just takes a bit of putting your foot down, albeit graciously and politely, to get things to go your way.

Q: My divorced parents are fighting over everything. I just want to elope! How do I make them stop all this?

A: Considering that my parents are divorced and my husband's parents are as well, we definitely had the potential for lots of fighting during our wedding plans. I'm sure it's the same with all brides and grooms with divorced parents. That worrying about potential parental fighting can cause enough stress for 100 brides.

If your divorced parents have always fought or been intolerant of each other in social situations, you're going to have to take the proverbial bull by the horns and raise the issue before it rears its ugly head. Sit your parents down and tell them this: While you and your fiancé understand that they are no longer married and may not like each other, they are still your parents and this day isn't about them. It's about you and your future spouse getting married. Let them know that you are on their side and know that the day could be potentially uncomfortable for them. But assure them that you won't put your parents in any awkward situations, such as the father-mother dance or having to stand next to each other in the receiving line. Tell them that you'll make arrangements with everything from the deejay to the table assignments to keep the pairs out of each other's way. Remind them that regardless of all the interference you'll attempt to run for them, nothing is 100 percent. So, should they find themselves standing near each other in the buffet line or a mother and stepmother waiting in the lavatory queue, you expect everyone to be on his or her best behavior.

This is supposed to be a happy day, not a day for fighting, and each of the divorced parents—and their respective spouses, if they've remarried—have got to put whatever beefs they have with each other in the back of their minds. Stress that you expect your parents to act respectfully and civilly to one another, and then end by saying this:

*If you don't think that you can do as I've asked,
I don't want you coming to my wedding.*

I know that's a hard statement to make, but you've got to make it clear to your parents that you want to spend your wedding day enjoying yourself and your guests. You don't want to have to be playing referee with your parents—or asking someone else to. Usually, when grown children give their parents that ultimatum, they do as they're asked and behave accordingly. Or they don't show up.

Q: My parents just announced that they're splitting up. What are the details I need to consider given this new and unexpected obstacle?

A: Talk about bad timing. I'm sorry to hear that your parents have separated, but that doesn't mean that you have to cancel your wedding. However, you may have to make a few small modifications to the wedding to make sure that the day runs smoothly.

First, have you sent out your invitations yet? If not, you may want to be sure to word them in a way that denotes that your parents are now considered to be separate entities. So instead of listing them as Mr. and Mrs. John Smith, you should list them as Mrs. Mary Smith and Mr. John Smith.

Second, did one of your parents leave because they were involved with someone else? If so, you need to have a heart-to-heart talk with that parent to explain that while he or she may have found someone new, your wedding is not the appropriate place to introduce that new squeeze to the rest of your family and friends—especially if the separation from your other parent is still very new and not everyone knows about it. Of course, this parent may not like what you have to say, so you've got to offer that parent two options: show up at your wedding, acting like the adult (and still married) person you've asked that parent to be, or, if that parent doesn't want to be near the soon-to-be ex or feels shunned because the new girlfriend/boyfriend isn't invited, then that parent needs to know not to come to the event. Yes, that's a hard position in which to put a parent, but sometimes parents who are no longer married need to be reminded, ad nauseam, that your wedding day isn't about them. It's not the time to announce a divorce or to introduce a new girlfriend or boyfriend. It's a day to celebrate their child who is getting married. And, again, if a parent cannot recognize that he or she is not the center of attention, then that parent may be better off not attending your wedding.

Let me tell you of a bride I knew who had a self-centered father who wanted to use his daughter's wedding not only to introduce his new girlfriend to everyone but also to announce that his new girlfriend was having a baby. The bride put her foot down about the whole girlfriend thing—especially because most of her family's social circle didn't even know her parents had split up—and guess what? Her dad showed up at her wedding—and solo no less—and was on his best behavior all day. He later confessed to his daughter that before she'd spoken up, he hadn't realized how much the split had bothered her. He figured that because she was an adult and living on her own, having her parents break up would be no big deal. Well, it was a big deal—and an even bigger deal because she was getting married. Because she was open about her feelings, she went on to have the wedding day of her dreams. And eventually she developed a cordial relationship with her father's girlfriend, who became his second wife.

Another way to make sure that things go your way with newly separated parents is to approach things the way you would with long-time divorced parents. That is, let them know that you are on their side and know that the day could be potentially uncomfortable for them. You also want to assure your parents that you won't do anything such as make them dance together or stand next to each other in the receiving line. However, do emphasize that while you'll do your best to run interference for them, you can't assure them that they won't end up standing next to each other at some point—nor should you have to. That said, say, in no uncertain terms, that you expect your parents to be on their best behavior and to act as cordially to each other as possible.

Q: My fiancé's parents are in the middle of getting a divorce, which is complicating all of our plans.

A: The best advice for dealing with difficult (and divorcing) parents bears repeating.

First, be sure to list those parents separately on invitations, in programs, and any other printed materials where their names might appear together. Also reiterate to your officiant, deejay, or anyone else who may be introducing the parents that your fiancé's parents are not to be referred to as Mr. and Mrs., but rather as John Smith and Mary Smith (or use the mother's maiden name if it is her wish).

Second, finagle seating arrangements, table assignments, and anything else that may occur on the big day so that once-married-but-now-split parents will not have to be near to each other. And do let those warring factions know the extent to which you will be rearranging things to make them more comfortable on your big day.

Third, despite all that you do to make things go perfectly, know that things can go wrong and do go wrong. So be up front with his parents about the possibility of any Murphy's Law mishaps at the wedding ceremony and reception, and tell them to be prepared for it—and to act like a grown-up should a plan go awry. For example, should the deejay goof and ask that the groom's parents dance together, tell them that you expect them to suck it up and do it for the happiness of their son.

Finally, have him tell his parents that if they don't think that they can act accordingly at the wedding, then they should just stay home. Usually this kind of ultimatum turns parents behaving badly into compliant people who needed a wake-up call to improve their behavior.

Wedding Wisdom

My dad's been married three times. I'm still in touch with his second wife, my ex-stepmother, and her two kids (my half siblings, ages 8 and 12). I wanted the kids in the wedding for a very personal reason: After my mother and father got divorced when I was 12, my favorite aunt hadn't invited me, my brother, and mother to her wedding because she thought it would be awkward. I understood, but always felt sad and left out—and promised I'd never let that happen to other children of divorce in my family. I wanted my stepsiblings to feel included in the rest of the family, even if our father was no longer married to their mother. However, I also knew that dad's third wife would flip out if the second wife was there. And I realized there was no way I could invite the kids from marriage number two without inviting wife number two. I agonized about this for a week or two. Then my fiancé said, 'This shouldn't be your problem.' He was right. I decided to invite everyone and let them work it out amongst themselves. I calmly announced to dad that I was inviting everyone— my mother (of course), my ex-stepmother, and dad's current wife, and that I would expect everyone to be accommodating. My stepsiblings were in the wedding and had a great time. Dad got to be there with all his kids, which he really liked. His wife came, and while my ex-stepmother bowed out of the wedding, she knew she was welcome and invited. I feel like I did the right thing.
—Christine, California

Q: I just sent out my invitations, including to some friends from work. Now my colleagues have found out that they're not invited to the wedding and things are feeling tense around the office.

A: It's always difficult dealing with a guest list when coworkers are involved. You can't always invite everyone you work with, and sometimes you just don't want to! The best way to avoid any tense situations at work is to avoid the problem before it happens. That is, as soon as you get engaged, let people know—either directly or by dropping hints in conversation—that you're going to be working with a tight budget or a small space and therefore won't be able to have as big of a wedding as you might like. This will let people know, in a subtle way, that they may not be invited to your wedding.

Of course, not everyone picks up on subtle clues. That's why, when it comes time to actually mail your wedding invitations, you should follow up your hint-dropping with direct conversations with each person you work with who might assume he or she is invited to the wedding but for reasons you needn't explain, wasn't. (Make sure you have these conversations before or as soon as the invitations go out. You want to nip any potential problems in the bud before the invited start receiving their invitations.)

Please do not send out a mass e-mail or voicemail to all of your colleagues, figuring that if you get the message out there, things will be okay. Instead, take the time to personally call, e-mail, or walk to each person's cubicle and say something such as, "I know you've probably heard me talking about my wedding plans, and I just wanted to let you know that I'm unable to extend an invitation to you. We have a really tight budget (or small chapel—or whatever reason you want to give, without delving into too much details) and there were so many people that I wanted to invite, including you, but I couldn't. I'm sure you'll understand." How could your coworker not understand, when you've handled the situation so graciously? And if for some reason your coworker gets offended, remember: You did the right thing and handled the situation directly and tactfully. If the coworker doesn't like it, it's his or her problem, not yours.

Q: My invitations went out last week and today I got fired. My boss, who fired me, is one of the people I invited, but now I don't want him at my wedding. Can I revoke his invitation?

A: I don't think you can ever revoke someone's invitation, but if you're lucky, your former boss is feeling as awkward as you are right now, and he'll decline the invitation. If he doesn't decline and decides to join you at your wedding, take the upper road and make sure that you act politely and graciously to him at your wedding. He'll be the one who'll have to explain to your guests exactly who he is and how it is that he's your former boss. That should make for interesting dinner conversation.

Chapter 4
Bridal Gown and Groom's Attire

Q: The shop where I ordered my wedding gown went out of business. Now I have no gown and, worst of all, my money is gone, too.

A: By chance, did you pay for your wedding gown by credit card? If so, you should dispute any charges from the wedding gown shop when they appear on your credit card statement. Thanks to the Fair Credit Billing Act, which the Federal Trade Commission enforces, you may not have to pay for "goods and services you didn't accept or weren't delivered as agreed." (Visit the Federal Trade Commission's Website at *www.ftc.gov* for more information about your rights as a consumer. Turn to page 35 for more information on the Fair Credit Billing Act.) Also, be sure to notify your local Better Business Bureau and state's Attorney General's office about this fly-by-night business so that, should the owners attempt to establish themselves elsewhere, you can warn others.

Now to the more immediate problem of your dress—or lack thereof. The good news is that you can definitely find another dress to wear at your wedding, depending on how flexible you're willing to be and how much time you have left before the big day.

If you have a couple of months before the wedding, you can go to another gown shop and order a similar dress to the one you originally chose. However, given what you've just been through, you may be more comfortable buying a dress from a shop that sells gowns off the rack. What does off the rack mean? That you literally are buying a dress from the rack in the store, not ordering it based on a sample you try on.

Call ahead to department stores with formal departments and bridal salons near you to find out if they have a decent off-the-rack dress selection. You don't want to waste your time going to stores that order dresses only.

Other places to find gowns off the rack include designer sample sales (check "sales and bargains" listings in your local paper or city magazine for such events), outlet stores, resale shops, and (believe it or not) prom dress stores—so many of today's special occasion dresses geared towards teenagers could easily double as wedding dresses. There's also a benefit to shopping in a junior's department: Many department stores realize that not every woman wears a size 2 or size 10, so there's usually a wide array of wedding-like dresses in range of sizes.

Another benefit to buying off the rack is that if you need to have alterations done, you can bring your dress to a tailor right away. You won't have to wait until the dress arrives to have your first fitting, and you can rest assured that you won't have any additional snafus with your gown.

Q: I called the bridal shop where I'd ordered my gown to ask them a question, and I discovered that my dress won't be ready in time because they forgot to order it. Now it's too late for them to get the dress I wanted.

A: First, I hope the shop owner apologized to you for this mishap. Then I hope that they offered to help you on your order by getting you another gown—and expedited—for no cost or at a discounted price. Or they should have offered to let you take a look at any off-the-rack gowns they might have in the store—and then offered to do alterations on that dress for free. Basically, I hope that the shop attempted to make good on their goof-up. If they didn't, then you should demand that they refund your money, and you should take your business elsewhere. While I understand that mistakes can happen, any business should try to make up for its mistake by making good on its promise in one way or another.

I spoke with a recent bride who, while shopping for her own dress, witnessed an argument between another bride-to-be and the bridal shop owner. As it turned out, the bridal shop had forgotten to order the dress and there was not enough time to order one. The irate bride remembered that the sample was close to her size and demanded that they give her the sample and order themselves a new sample. Not only did the shop agree to this notion, but her alterations and veil were free of charge. If all else fails, and you're lucky enough to have a sample close to your size (not too small of course), this option may be your last resort in a tight spot.

Tips for Getting a Gown in a Pinch

Now as far as getting the dress that you need, if the gown shop isn't willing to work with you, then you'll need to explore your options for buying a dress off the rack. These include:

- Calling bridal shops to see if they have off-the-rack dresses available (not all do). Many may not advertise that they do—these gowns are usually returns and not brand new—but if you call first, you may be surprised by what you find out.
- Finding out when designers may be holding sample or trunk sales in your area.
- Determining if a bridal designer has an outlet store near you.
- Visiting resale and consignment shops, especially those that benefit a good cause or are situated in a well-to-do area (meaning you'll likely get high-end castoffs at a bargain price).
- Asking friends, relatives, or even theater costume shops if they have a wedding gown you can borrow or rent.
- Checking out so-called "prom dresses" and other white or off-white formal wear in your local department store to see if you can find a gown that could double as a wedding dress. Macy's stores nationwide may no longer sell bridal gowns (neither does JCPenney and Bloomingdale's), but they have plenty of special occasion dresses that can pinch-hit for a gown. For example, at JCPenney many of the off-the-rack bridesmaid dresses come in white and look just like wedding gowns.

❀ Visiting a bridal store that advertises its in-stock wedding gowns, such as David's Bridal. The store's Website at *www.davidsbridal.com* can refer you to a location nearby.

Q: A pipe burst in the bridal shop where I bought my gown, and I just found out that my dress is ruined.

A: Is there enough time for the bridal shop to order you another gown? Does the store happen to have another location where they might have dresses in stock you can try on? Don't give up hope on replacing the dress of your dreams until you've exhausted all of your options. It's possible that the shop's insurance will cover the damage from the broken pipe and work with the shop to replace the inventory pronto. Or the shop owner may be able to work out a deal with the dress manufacturer to have a replacement expedited so you'll have the same dress you ordered delivered in time. Find out first what the bridal shop can do to help you before looking for a dress elsewhere. Then, if all else fails, you're going to have to get a new dress. Turn to page 51 for my Tips for Getting a Gown in a Pinch.

Finally, because you can't control when bad things happen to good dresses (and other things related to your wedding), you may want to look into buying a wedding insurance policy to cover your event. One company, called WedSafe (*www.wedsafe.com*), came to fruition after an engaged couple couldn't find any brokers offering insurance to protect their wedding day festivities and all the things that went into the plans—including attire, rings, and vendors who don't show up. Like other kinds of insurance policies, you'll pay a nominal fee for a wedding insurance plan (less than $400), but that fee will cover damages adding up to more than $60,000.

Q: My gown just came in and it doesn't fit. How could this happen?

A: It's rare to have a gown fit a bride perfectly the minute she tries it on. That's why most bridal shops come complete with seamstresses or tailors to make alterations on the dress. So if your dress looks weird on you because it's too big, don't worry—you'd be amazed at what a few well-placed alterations can do.

However, is it more than just a little big? Did the bridal dress shop actually order your dress in the wrong size—either too small or too big? Or did you lose or gain so much weight that the size you ordered will no longer work?

If we're talking about the former situation, where the gown shop goofed and ordered the wrong size, then they should fix the problem for free. They should either expedite the ordering of a gown in the correct size or give you a refund. Don't let them talk you into altering a too-big dress to fit you—most smart seamstresses know that you can only take a piece of clothing down a size or two before you change the look of the garment so much that it no longer looks natural. So don't try this with your dress—especially not your wedding dress. I'd hate to have you end up with a dress that fits but looks terrible because of all the cutting and sewing that had to be done.

Now if you've lost or gained weight so that the dress no longer fits, you've got a couple of options. You can either put on or take off the same amount of weight that affected your being able to wear the dress. If you've lost weight—but not a bunch of dress sizes—maybe you can have the dress altered. If you've gained so much weight that losing enough weight to fit back into the dress is not an option, see if the dress shop will work with you to either give you a partial refund or apply the cost of the dress to another dress. (I don't think this is too much to ask for—I'm guessing that they've seen plenty of brides with fluctuating weights.)

Of course, if you don't have enough time to order or alter the dress that no longer fits, then you're going to have to buy a dress off the rack. (Turn to page 51 for my Tips for Getting a Gown in a Pinch.)

Q: I love to dance and I'm afraid that my dress is going to rip if I dance too much. But I definitely want to dance at my wedding. What should I do?

A: First, you should find some comfort in the fact that most wedding gowns are sturdily constructed garments that are designed to stand up to a day's worth of activity—ranging from walking down the aisle to dancing the night away. So chances are your dress is going to be just fine—that is, unless you decide to start break dancing on the dance floor.

Regardless of your dancing style, it's a good bet to keep a sewing kit on hand, not only for your peace of mind but also for your guests' peace of mind, should they tear their clothing. I would recommend stocking each bathroom at the reception with a full sewing kit—thread, needles, various buttons, etc.—along with other necessities that a bride or her guests might need at the last minute. These would include tampons, sanitary pads, panty hose, hairspray, deodorant, clear nail polish (for panty hose runs), nail glue, and breath mints. If you're inviting children to your reception, you may also want to add diapers and wipes to your list of necessities.

Q: I tried my gown on at home and then spilled coffee on it.

A: I can just imagine what led to this disaster: You were so excited about your upcoming wedding that you just *had* to have your dress hanging in your bedroom so you could gaze lovingly upon it in the days before your wedding. I was a bride once, too, and I know how exciting it is to have the perfect dress. You can't take your eyes off of it and, like a little girl playing dress up, you probably tried it on multiple times each day and modeled it in front of a full-length mirror. Again, I know, because I did it too and in hindsight I know I shouldn't have been so flippant with my dress. It's an expensive garment and one that has to look just right on the big day. Then while you were wearing it, you probably got distracted—perhaps the phone rang?—and while you were chatting away on the phone, you unthinkingly picked up your cup of coffee and, before you knew it, you'd spilled it on yourself.

First let me say—don't feel so bad. These kinds of things happen to many brides. I know a bride who took her gown home early from the bridal store, and she did everything right—she hung it on her closet door, didn't touch it, and was as careful as she could have been with the dress. But she didn't keep the protective cover on the dress like the bridal shop owner had suggested, and she didn't stop to think about the other members of her family. One day her mom was walking by her room and decided she wanted to give the gown an up-close inspection. Well, on the way in the door to her daughter's room, she tripped. As luck would have it, Mom was holding a cup of coffee, which went flying from her hands and landed smack-dab in the middle of the closet door—where her daughter's dress was hanging. Before her mom could do anything, the coffee spilled all the way down the front of the dress. I also know brides who tried on their gowns—then stopped for a snack and well, you know, spilled their food on themselves. I've also heard of brides trying on their dresses and being extremely careful the whole time they have it on, only to smear makeup all over the gown as they took it off over their head.

So you see, spilling coffee on a wedding dress really isn't as uncommon as you think, and I hope hearing that makes you feel a bit better about what happened. Now let's get to the issue at hand—your halfway ruined dress.

Believe it or not, your wedding isn't ruined—perhaps only your dress is. But then again, your dress outlook may not be so dire—there are a number of solutions to consider for fixing this situation and your dress.

I suggest you start by calling the bridal shop where you bought the dress and telling them what happened. (If you're too embarrassed to do so, maybe your mom could make the initial call—unless she's the one who spilled the coffee like the klutzy mom I previously mentioned. Or, better yet, you could enlist your maid of honor. Isn't this the sort of thing maids of honor sign up to do?) The store may be able to call your dress manufacturer and rush order a new dress. (Of course, you'll have to pay for this new dress, so if you've got an unlimited budget, go for this option first.) Also, if the coffee destroyed the entire dress, this may be your only option if you want the same dress again.

If your budget is getting tighter and only an easy-to-fix portion of the dress got ruined—say, the skirt—call the dress shop or the manufacturer directly and order extra fabric. Then you can have a seamstress redo the bottom of the dress and any adornment. Of course, all of this will be a snap to pull off if there's enough time to make it happen and the shop has a seamstress on call that can work a last-minute job. I know a Colorado bridal shop owner who had a customer who needed to quick-fix a ruined dress—and with only a week to go before the wedding, this shop owner was able to arrange to have the entire dress redone. Keep in mind that this bride had to pay extra to fix this mistake—and you will too.

If redoing the dress won't work, cleaning it may be your next best option. Start by asking your bridal shop for a referral to a reputable dry cleaner. If that doesn't work, call around to local dry cleaners and find out which ones specialize in not only cleaning wedding gowns, but also getting rid of food stains. Look for a dry cleaner that does its cleaning on the premises. This is for one simple reason: With limited time to get the job done, you don't want to add in any other factors—such as shipping your dress to another location to be cleaned—that might cause your dress to get lost or to be further damaged.

Now let's say that the cleaner *can* clean the dress so that you don't smell like the inside of a Starbucks, but the dress is not back to its original color—there's just no hiding the brownish stain that spread across the skirt. A quick cover-up solution to consider would be dyeing the dress. Sure, you may have had your heart set on a white or off-white dress, but perhaps you should learn to love the idea of a sepia-colored dress that would make you look so fashion forward and would do an awesome job of covering up the stain.

If dyeing the dress just won't cut if for you and if the silhouette of the dress would allow for it, you could hire a seamstress to construct an overlay for the skirt in a semi-sheer or other colored fabric that would hide the stain.

Finally, if you discover that no amount of time, money, manpower, or creative covering-up can salvage your ruined dress, you're going to have to get a new one. (See page 51 for Tips for Getting a Gown in a Pinch.)

Q: What if my shoes get ruined or break at the wedding?

A: Want to know what's great about a wedding gown? It's usually very long and no one sees your feet anyway. (I know plenty of brides who sported tennis shoes or white sneakers on their big day, and no one was the wiser.) So if your shoes get ruined, you break a heel, or if the darn things just become too uncomfortable for you to bear, take them off. Maybe you could even treat yourself to a new pair of white Keds, which you can decorate to match your dress. Then you can bring them along to put on when you feel like your feet need a rest.

Q: My dress came in, and I tried it on, and I just started to cry. It's uncomfortable, and I hate the way it looks on me. What do I do now?

A: Were you one of the unlucky brides who could not try on a sample of her dress because you don't have a model-sized body? I was one of them too, and I've been with many of my similarly shaped friends when they've tried on gowns—or rather, held gowns up to themselves because they couldn't actually put them on. If there was one thing I would change about the bridal gown industry, it would be the practice of only stocking gown samples in one or, if you're lucky, a few sizes. As everyone knows, different women come in different sizes, and you shouldn't be penalized for being a size 2 or a size 12 by not being able to try your wedding gown on first. (Most gowns are stocked in sample size 6 or 8, so really tiny brides are at as big a disadvantage as the plus-size ones are!)

Fine. I'll get off my soapbox now and address your very real (and very emotional) problem—you hate your dress. I don't mean to belittle your feelings, but could it be that you hate your dress simply because you're not used to seeing yourself in such a formal-looking article of clothing? There have been many times in my life when I've bought something expensive and important (two qualities I would apply to a wedding gown) and at first I hated them. Why? Because they were new and very different from the kinds of things I normally wear or from how I'm comfortable with myself looking. By giving myself a few days to get accustomed to these new items, I grew to like them and to appreciate how different they made me look.

Is it possible for you to give yourself a few days to do the same? Why don't you have a friend take a photograph of you in your dress? Then you can keep that photograph with you and refer to it often. After a couple of days, see if your opinion about your dress has changed. My guess is the more you see how gorgeous you look in your wedding gown, the more you're going to like the image of yourself as a bride.

Now let's say that you've given it a few days and you still hate the dress—or you can't get over the fact that it was so uncomfortable because of the fabric. Talk to the bridal shop owner and see if you can't work something out. Will they take the dress back and give you a credit for it that you can apply to another dress they can order? Are there any off-the-rack dresses in the shop that you can try on so you won't have to order yet another dress that you've never seen yourself wearing? Be sure to focus on dresses that are made of soft fabrics or ones that won't rub you the wrong way (literally) so you don't end up with another uncomfortable dress. Don't give up. If you keep looking—especially now that you know what you don't like—I'm confident you'll find the dress of your dreams.

Q: While I was trying on my gown at the bridal shop, I needed to use the ladies room. I couldn't believe how hard it was to maneuver the stall in this gigantic gown. What am I supposed to do on my wedding day? Hold it in?

A: A bride I know faced this exact situation on her wedding day. Because she was wearing a huge hoop-skirted dress, her first trip to the bathroom was almost traumatic—she had to turn sideways to get into the toilet, she couldn't figure out how to lift up her dress, and then she couldn't see the toilet to sit down on it. Luckily, her matron of honor had worn a similar kind of dress to her wedding and had the whole big dress/bathroom thing down pat. What was the solution? The bride had to straddle the toilet—you know, squat over it like your mom always told you to do in public restrooms. (You may even need to face the wall so that the back of the dress doesn't get in the way—all you need to do is pick up the front.) Well, when it comes to a huge wedding gown, that advice comes in handy. Anyway, that's what this bride ended up doing and while she felt like a complete idiot in the process (thank goodness no one could see her), she was able to get her business done and get back to her wedding in no time. I'd suggest that you practice the straddle/squatting thing as well so that when you've got to go on your big day, you know exactly what to do.

Another suggestion: If you have a huge dress on, go with garters and stockings instead of panty hose. That way you won't have to get completely undressed just to pee.

Q: I took my gown home a week early and my pet decided to "welcome" my dress. Now it's ruined. What can I do with only one week to go before my wedding?

A: How simple or how difficult it is to fix your dress depends on how badly your pet ruined your dress—and where it made it's mark. Did your bird roost and poop on a shoulder? Chances are a good dry cleaner might be able to get the stain out. Did your cat sharpen its claws or did your dog chew on the skirt? You may be able to hide the damage by bringing your dress to a seamstress and having her create a skirt overlay to go over the original skirt, thus hiding the hole your pet created. Was it the bodice that got destroyed? If you're lucky enough to have chosen a dress with patchwork-looking material, you may be able to patch the hole successfully. But if your pet did more damage than the most talented seamstress could ever fix, probably your only option is to buy a new dress. And with only a week before the big day, you'll have your best luck with an off-the-rack dress. Please turn to page 51 for Tips for Getting a Gown in a Pinch.

> ### Wedding Wisdom
>
> At our wedding reception, this very young waiter served me first. We had roast beef in hunter sauce, and as he moved to put the plate on the table, it tipped and brown gravy spilled all down the front of my dress. The poor waiter turned deathly pale and started babbling that he'd get the catering manager, the restaurant manager—anyone who would keep me from self-destructing. Fortunately, my friend Brenda, who had made my dress, was one of my bridesmaids and was sitting right beside me and knew what to do. She had the catering manager bring over a towel and a giant bottle of club soda, and within two minutes the dress was as good as new, and the waiter looked mightily relieved.
> —Laura, Ontario, Canada

Q: I'm a habitual bargain shopper, and even though I've already ordered my dress, I continued shopping around and found the same dress for a much cheaper price. What should I do?

A: What's your commitment with the bridal shop where you originally ordered your dress? Have you paid for the whole thing up front? Or did you have to pay a deposit only? Would it be cheaper for you in the long run to risk losing the deposit to pay for this other dress? In other words, is there a significant difference between the deposit (which the shop will likely not refund to you) and the price of the new dress? In my way of thinking, if you were going to pay $3,000 for a gown, and you only had to put 10 percent down (or $300) and then you found the same dress for $1,000, you'll still have saved $1,700 on the dress, even if you forfeit the deposit. However, if the savings is less than a deposit or any money that you might lose by canceling the order, then I say it's not worth the hassle. Of course, you can always call the dress shop and find out what their cancellation policy is. Maybe you'll be able to get all of your money back. Maybe you'll only lose the deposit. But find out first what risk you face by changing your dress order. Saving a couple of bucks may not be worth the hassle in the long run.

Q: The formalwear shop where we ordered the tuxedos is dark and boarded up, and no one is answering the phone. That means the groom and the groomsmen have nothing to wear and, worst of all, our deposit is gone.

A: The risk of losing a cash deposit is why I always advise brides and grooms (and anyone else who is making purchases) to pay by credit card whenever possible. You've got to remember that you've got the law on your side when you pay with plastic—specifically the Fair Credit Billing Act of 1974 (see pages 35-36 for details).

This act protects consumers against unauthorized credit card charges or, in the case of a couple hiring vendors for a wedding, "charges for goods and services [that] weren't delivered as agreed," according to the Federal Trade Commission (FTC) Website at *www.ftc.gov*. (The FTC enforces the Fair Credit Billing Act.) What that means is if a vendor promises to cater, photograph, or play music at your wedding—or in your case, deliver tuxedos for all the men in the wedding party, including the groom—and then doesn't do as promised, you can report that violation to the FTC and use the criteria of the Fair Credit Billing Act to sue the unreliable vendor. (You can get the details on how to file a violation on the FTC Website.)

In addition to the Fair Credit Billing Act and paying by credit card, you can also cover yourself financially by purchasing a wedding insurance plan. For example, one wedding insurance company offers four different policy levels that will cover lost or damaged attire costing between $1,000 and $3,000, and it may cover you in the event that a formal wear shop goes out of business before you can pick up your attire.

So you know how to get your money back. Now on to the more pressing matter: dressing your men. Your best bet is to find a formalwear shop that stocks tuxedos on site (versus a shop that orders each ensemble from a wholesaler to fulfill an order). Look on the Internet or in the Yellow Pages for formalwear shops near you that advertise with phrases such as "All Inventory on Premises" or "Same-Day Services." Be sure to call or e-mail to confirm that this means that they can get you a range of tuxedo styles and sizes as soon as you need them.

Q: We called the formalwear shop where we ordered the tuxedo rentals to ask them a question, and we discovered that they'd forgotten to order all of the tuxedos we need. We have some pretty "hefty" ushers who need special-ordered tuxes. What can we do?

A: Before you panic, find out if the shop can expedite the special-ordered tuxes—and encourage them to pick up the extra cost of this measure, because it was their mistake that got you into this situation. If they refuse, see if you can cancel your order with the original shop—and let them know that you're willing to do so—and take your business elsewhere.

To find a formalwear shop that can fit all of your groomsmen, big and small, you need to employ the same strategies as someone who suddenly found that the shop where they'd placed their order had gone out business. (See page 61.)

Start by finding a formalwear shop that stocks tuxedos on site (versus a shop that orders each ensemble from a wholesaler to fulfill an order)—and also offers "big and tall" sizes as well as "athletic cut" (for the more muscular build). Look on the Internet or in the Yellow Pages for formalwear shops near you that advertise with phrases such as "All Inventory on Premises" or "Same-Day Services." Be sure to call or e-mail to confirm that this means that they can get you a range of tuxedo styles and sizes as soon as you need them. If you find that they can't dress your "larger" groomsmen, call around to stores that serve the "big and tall" and athletic clientele and find out if they can recommend a formalwear shop. You may discover that they have a formalwear division on premises—which means you may end up having to dress your male attendants from two different shops. But at least this way everyone in the wedding party will have the attire they need to look great on your wedding day.

Q: I found out that the formalwear shop where we're getting the tuxedoes is overcharging us big time. I want to cancel the order but they're telling me I can't.

𝒜: Does the formalwear shop you're using advertise in the Yellow Pages, newspaper, or local coupon saver? Any chance you found them because they offered a "we'll beat anyone's price" offer in their advertisement? If so, do you have something printed from another formalwear shop that shows how out of line this shop's prices are? With this evidence in hand, you should bring this original promise to the shop's attention—and then let them know that you'll be notifying the local Better Business Bureau and state's Attorney General's office (which tracks fair practices among businesses and consumers) about their refusal to honor their promise.

Even if the shop never offered to beat a competitors price—and you didn't sign any agreement with them stating that your order was non-refundable and cannot be cancelled—you should tell the local Better Business Bureau and state's Attorney General's office about this shop's decision not to be flexible with you. Perhaps by notifying the shop that you'll be discussing your situation with higher authorities, they'll lower their prices to be more in line with the going rate or let you out of your agreement. I'm not suggesting that you use extortion to get a better deal, but you should do everything in your means not to let this business rip you off.

Chapter 5
Wedding Accessories and Bridesmaid Attire

Q: I got these great looking shoes to match my dress, but now I realize they hurt my feet. Can I walk down the aisle barefoot?

A: Unless you're getting married on the beach, I don't think you can get away with being a shoeless bride. But I also don't think that you should wear shoes that are uncomfortable, or you're going to be miserable your entire wedding day. I'd say definitely invest in another pair of shoes, and make sure that you follow this long-standing advice for finding shoes that fit—always shop for shoes at the end of or late in the day when your feet are likely to be most swollen and tired. If a pair of shoes feels comfortable at 5 p.m., you're pretty much guaranteed that they'll also be comfortable earlier in the day.

Another option to consider: Buy a couple of different pairs of shoes, and see which one you end up liking the most—as far as looks and feel goes. Of course, don't wear the shoes on a non-carpeted surface or you'll scuff the bottoms and won't be able to return them. And, it goes without saying that you should make sure ahead of time that the store where you bought the shoes will let you take them back. You don't want to end up with five pairs of wedding shoes in the end, or a huge shopping debt because you couldn't return any of these shoes.

If you bought dyeable shoes (or nondyeable, for that matter) and can't return them, consider that if they comfortably fit a friend, they can be dyed to the friend's liking and all your diligent shopping will not go to waste.

Q: I found the perfect shoes for my bridesmaids to wear and bought them for everyone. Then I found them cheaper somewhere else. Should I bring the original ones back?

A: Please tell me that you haven't dyed the original pairs yet and that you weren't planning to try to return shoes that will match your bridesmaid dresses only. It goes without saying that you shouldn't commit to a pair of dyeable shoes until you know that they're comfortable on everyone and that you're confident that you've paid the best price.

You can absolutely try to return the original shoes, but don't be surprised if the store refuses to take them back. Given the very nature of dyeable shoes—and the fact that the shop may be wary that you've already done some dyeing to them—you may find yourself dealing with a "no returns" policy. If you found shoes that are not dyeable that match the dresses perfectly, a return policy is also quite important— shoes that specifically match a dress can be a costly investment! So you've got to figure out if you can even return the shoes and, more importantly, if the cost savings you've discovered is really worth the time and effort it will take to return the shoes. I would think that you have enough on your plate already, and finding the best deal on bridesmaid shoes, after you've already secured perfectly good footwear for your attendants, is stress you don't need. Once you've found something that makes you happy, please stop shopping around. Learn to live with your decision and move on.

Q: I need to wear a strapless bra with my gown and left the shopping for it to the last minute. Now I can't find one. Can I go braless on the big day?

A: Well, it really depends on what your dress looks like, how well it holds you in, and how well endowed you are. My guess is if you're wearing a dress with a bodice that could double as a bustier, you're probably fine going without a bra. The same notion applies if you have a small chest and your dress is quite fitted. However, without seeing your dress, knowing its construction, or even having any idea what your body type is, it's hard for me to give you an unwavering thumbs-up or thumbs-down to the notion of going braless. I think your best bet is to call the shop where you bought your dress and explain your predicament. The salespeople there have a tremendous amount of experience fitting brides into gowns, and they are probably better people to advise you on whether you need to find a bra or whether you can get away without it. Better yet, the shop may be able to special order or rush ship a strapless bra that would go perfectly with your dress. Many bridal shops will also sew cups into or even transform an existing bra (cut the back and straps) to be sewn into the gown, so ask the shop's seamstress what she can do for you.

Q: I forgot to pack panties and now it looks like I'm going to have to go commando on my wedding day. What do I do when we do the garter toss?

A: Unless you're getting married in the middle of nowhere, there's got to be a 24-hour store nearby that has an underwear aisle. I realize the idea of wearing a pair of generic white cotton underwear on your wedding day probably doesn't fit with your image of yourself as a bride, but you probably don't want your guests seeing what isn't under your dress, if you will, if you decide to forego your underwear. You may think you can get away without it, but you're sure to have a situation where you'll wish you had something on under your dress. Case in point: I know a bride who had a midsummer night's wedding, and, boy, was it hot! She couldn't fathom the idea of wearing panty hose on such a hot evening, so she wore white knee-highs instead. She looked great walking down the aisle, sharing her first dance with her husband, and no one was the wiser of her hosiery choice—until it came time to toss the garter. When she sat down in that chair and lifted her dress slightly so her husband could get her garter off, the secret of her knee-highs was out of the box—and captured on film. Now every time this woman looks at her wedding photos, she's reminded of her panty hose shortcut with the picture of her sitting there in her gorgeous gown with a pair of knee-highs on. Don't let yourself get caught in a similar situation and cut corners on your undergarments. Even if you've got to put on a pair of "granny panties," do it. You won't regret it.

Q: The underwear that I thought would be great under my dress is uncomfortable and is giving me panty lines. I don't want to wear it.

A: First, you have to ask yourself if the panty lines are worse than the uncomfortable underwear or vice versa. Why? Because if it's the panty lines that are really going to bother you on the big day, I'd say bite the bullet and buy yourself a thong. While this form of underwear may not be my favorite, it does do the trick with preventing panty lines. Or if thongs aren't your thing, invest in a pair of panties that promise not to have panty lines. (Look for phrases on the tag such as "barely there" or "no seams." These are usually made of a smooth fabric and have very thin elastic, if any, around the edges so you won't see any lines under your dress.) If it's the discomfort more than the aesthetics of panty lines that is getting to you, definitely invest in a new pair of underwear that you're sure will feel comfortable. I don't condone brides going commando at their wedding, but I also don't condone brides being uncomfortable for the sake of fashion. There's no reason you have to be Miss Fancy Pants by wearing an expensive pair of "wedding" underwear that also happens to be horribly uncomfortable. Go with your everyday knickers if you'll feel better and more confident about your undergarment decision.

Q: The place from which we ordered the bridesmaid dresses won't have the dresses ready on time. Some lackey forgot to put in the order. Now what!?

A: Pardon the pun, but how wedded are you to these specific bridesmaid dresses that you chose? Could you find stand-ins somewhere else instead?

First and foremost, make sure that the original bridal shop gives you a full refund for the order they messed up on. Did you or your individual bridesmaids pay by credit card? I hope so, because they'll likely not have to pay for the charges because the dress shop didn't hold up its end of the deal. Paying by credit card is one of the smartest moves you can make when planning a wedding—especially when a vendor such as a bridal shop doesn't order the dress on time, orders the wrong dress, or, heaven forbid, closes shop before you can pick up your attire. (That's because the Fair Credit Billing Act of 1974 protects consumers who pay by credit card from having to pay for goods or services that weren't delivered as promised.See page 35 for more information.)

If a refund isn't possible, then firmly ask the shop's owner to make good on their mistake by providing you with a rushed order to replace the dresses or discounts on off-the-rack replacements.

If you've got enough time and you truly love the dresses you ordered, find another bridal wear shop (one with a good reputation for hiring on-the-ball employees) and order the same dresses. Or call the dress manufacturer directly to see if they can't help you track down stores nearby with those dresses in stock.

If you can go the off-the-rack route and completely change your notion of what your bridesmaids should wear. Go to a department store that sells cocktail dresses or something similar, and pick out dresses in your preferred color. This will give your maids the option of getting a dress that they can truly wear again—such as to a formal event for work, New Year's Eve party, or, believe it or not, as a guest at someone else's wedding.

Finally, a creative option for bridesmaid dresses that offers the most flexibility is this: Choose a color that you want everyone to wear and then let each maid buy her own style dress in that color. I've seen wedding parties that use this approach, and it has a lovely effect. There will be women in full-length dresses, sweater sets and skirts, and cocktail dresses. It's a way to let the individuality of each maid shine through without asking them to pay for and wear a dress that will likely spend the rest of its days hanging in their closet.

> ### Wedding Wisdom
>
> *I went to pick up the bridesmaid dresses, and when they presented me with light blue and mint green polka-dot dresses, I about fainted. When I told them that they had ordered the wrong dresses, they informed me 'too bad, it's only six weeks until the wedding, we can't get the right ones in time.' I informed them that I was not having a polka-dot wedding and they had better get on the phone and find four dresses in the colors and sizes that I wanted. Sure enough, they came through.*
> *—Roberta, Indiana*

Q: Even though we've ordered the bridesmaid dresses, two of my bridesmaids have decided to go on a diet. They've already lost 10 pounds—and look great—but I'm afraid that the dresses won't work for them anymore once they come in.

A: First things first, be sure to compliment your bridesmaids on their weight loss, however big, small, or seemingly inconvenient it may be to you and your dress situation. As someone who lost a significant amount of weight at one time, I know what a big undertaking it can be to finally drop pounds, so be sure to tell them how proud you are of them and how great they look.

Then once you've got the compliments out of your system, get down to the dilemma at hand. Talk to your maids and to the dress shop where you ordered the gowns about your concern. Tell them that you're worried that the dresses they ordered may end up coming in too big. See if the dress shop can recommend a seamstress who can take in the dresses—and how much she can take them in without ruining the look of the dress. Maybe you'll get lucky and find out that the maids ordered their dresses a size too small—something I would never recommend, but which, in this case, will work perfectly. If so, then the dresses may fit them perfectly when they come in or may just need a small nip and tuck here and there.

Worst-case scenario? The dresses are way too big and no amount of alterations can fix them. Then you'll need to have your maids rush order new dresses in the correct sizes. Or they'll have to buy dresses off the rack somewhere.

Q: Some of our attendants live out of state and cannot be present for fittings.

A: Most of today's weddings include people who must travel from point A to point B to attend a wedding, and my guess is most bridal and formalwear shops are used to dealing with long-distance fitting situations. What I would recommend is making sure you let the shop know well in advance that some of the attendants will not be present for fittings and that you'll need to supply measurements by either fax, phone, e-mail, or ground mail. For example, a man can get measured at a tuxedo shop near him and then send the measurements to the shop the groom is working with—or to the groom himself. Bridesmaids can get fitted at a store near them, send their measurements to the bride, and then she can arrange for any last-minute alterations with a tailor.

Now if the bride or groom happens to be working with a chain store, it's possible to enter the measurements electronically in a shop in, say, California and have the shop in Connecticut (where the couple lives) bring them up on their system. Of course, check ahead to make sure that the shop is okay working this way.

Worst-case scenario if you can't figure out how to fit in fittings for out-of-state attendants? Change their attire. Instead of matching tuxedos, have your male attendants wear complementing suits. Approach things similarly with your bridesmaids. That is, forego the matching dresses and instead get dresses that go together. That way your long-distance attendants have more latitude in choosing their outfits—and you won't be left trying to coordinate long-distance fittings.

Q: The dresses are chosen and paid for, and my maid of honor just announced that she's pregnant. I want all of my maids to wear matching dresses, but I don't think the style I've picked comes in a maternity version.

A: Are you sure it doesn't come in a maternity version? With today's bride inching up in age into the late 20s and 30s, it's not unheard of for her to have attendants who have already had children—or are in the process of having kids. So what does that mean for you? You may be pleasantly surprised to find out that manufacturers are actually making maternity versions of their bridesmaid dresses.

Before you get down to the nitty-gritty of dress shopping, though, have a heart-to-heart talk with your maid of honor. Find out when she's due to have her baby, and if it's within a month or so of your wedding date, you should let her off the hook of her maid of honor duties. While most babies are born nearly on time, some come early and some come late. There is always the slight chance that your maid of honor could be in labor, at the hospital giving birth, or just home with her new baby by the time your big day rolls around. Or her baby could be late and she could be a full nine months pregnant and feeling quite large on your wedding date—and frankly as someone who's been pregnant twice, I know how incredibly uncomfortable it is to be nine months pregnant and have to put on a fancy dress and stand around at a wedding. Even though you give her an out, she may insist on fulfilling her maid-of-honor duties. But know in the back of your head that she may have to bow out at the last minute, due to contractions, a C-section, or simply being uncomfortable.

So, okay, your pregnant friend will still be your maid of honor. Where do you find her a dress that will fit her pregnant body? I think the easiest thing to do is to avoid the traditional maid-of-honor dress and let her buy something from a maternity shop that will be comfortable for her to wear and still fit in with your bridesmaid color scheme. Also, it may add a lovely touch to your wedding party to have your maid of honor wearing something slightly different from the other bridesmaids. I'm sure your mom-to-be maid of honor will appreciate having the traditional dress code lifted for her so she can look and feel great on your special day.

If your friend is due just before the wedding you may have the option of talking with the shop owner about ordering the same dress for her that you did for the other attendants, but *many* sizes too large for her. Find out if the size of her dress can be switched on the original order (there may be a fee). Keep in mind that all parts of a dress can be taken in, but there is only so much a dress can be let out. Most seamstresses can do last-minute fittings with as little time as a week to go before the wedding. (Giving the new mom a little time before being fitted allows for any belly shrinking or weight loss that may occur between the birth and the wedding.)

Q: I want my attendants to wear lavender, but two of them are refusing. They say that lavender makes them look all washed out. Why can't they cooperate with my wishes?

A: Anyone who agrees to be in someone's wedding party needs to understand one simple principle—by being a bridesmaid or maid of honor, you are deferring to the bride's taste on everything, from hairstyles to shoes to fashion statements. If your attendants don't seem to appreciate this little fact, then you need to have a little chat.

Without seeming like too much of a demanding bride, you should start out by telling these ladies how much it means to you to have them be in your wedding party and to stand up with you as you marry your true love. At the same time, though, you need to remind them that this is your wedding day, and that if you deferred to everyone's opinion on every little item, you'd never be able to make any decision or get anything done. So while you understand that lavender may not be their favorite color, it is yours and the one you chose for your wedding. Remind them that you would like all of your maids to be wearing the same hue, and if they can't put their personal distaste for lavender aside, then maybe they shouldn't be in the wedding. Tell them that you'll understand if they want to step aside and that you'll respect their decision if they do. Give them a short time line to let you know their decision, such as a week. Hopefully these ladies will be good enough friends to realize that bowing out of your wedding over something as silly as the color of the bridesmaid dresses really isn't worth it, and they'll end up wearing the lavender dresses that you prefer.

Q: I was very careful to pick inexpensive yet pretty dresses for all of my attendants—the maid of honor, my bridesmaids, and the flower girl. Now some of the people in my wedding party are refusing to pay for their dresses, citing budgetary reasons. How can they do this to me?

A: Did you really choose affordable dresses—so affordable that if push comes to shove you could pick up the tab for everyone in your wedding party? If the price of the dresses is really causing a problem for those involved—and sometimes it's really hard to know from the outside looking in the exact kinds of financial straits that certain people really are in—then the right thing for you to do is to buy everyone's dresses for them. Think about it this way—traditionally, the bride buys a gift for each of the people in her wedding party. Instead of loading them down with another knick-knack or bottle of perfume or piece of jewelry that they may not actually need, give them possibly the best gift you can—paying for the dresses you've asked them to wear to be in your wedding. Find some wiggle room in your budget to make this gesture a reality, and I'm confident that no one will complain about the dresses (or their price tag) from now until the day of your wedding. If anything they'll all be singing your praises for being the most generous bride ever.

Chapter 6
The Wedding Party

Q: Help! My maid of honor "quit" the wedding.

A: While I'm sure that you're disappointed that your friend no longer can or doesn't want to be in your wedding party, it really isn't the end of the world. Was she your only attendant? If so, is there someone else that you're equally close to that you could ask to be your maid of honor instead? If you have a big wedding party, is there someone you could elevate to maid of honor from bridesmaid? Perhaps one of your sisters could step in instead? I would always recommend choosing family over friends for such last-minute substitutions because, as you know, they say that blood is thicker than water. And when it comes to weddings, family members tend not to feel slighted if you choose them second or you're using them to fill a vacancy.

With that logic in mind, it would seem to make the most sense to choose a friend over a family member—simply because a family member probably wouldn't be insulted to be passed over. However, here's what I've learned in all my years of writing about weddings. Friends come and go but family will always be there for you. So you may have a best friend whom you absolutely can't live without right now, but chances are you may not be friends in a few years. Whereas your sister is there for you now and she'll be there for you in the future as well. Also, because friends do come and go, think about looking back at your wedding photos 10 or 20 years from now. Whom do you want to be standing there next to you as your maid of honor—a friend who may or may not be a friend in the future or the sister you grew up with? Only you will know the right person to choose to be your fill-in maid of honor, but do keep these notions in mind as you make your decision.

Q: One of my bridesmaids told me she no longer wants to be in the wedding. What do I do now?

A: I'm sure that your first reaction was probably, "How could she do this to me?" But trust me—this is a blessing in disguise. Having her back out of the wedding now is much better than having her stay in the wedding party and making your life miserable. And I'm guessing that any attendant who becomes a bridesmaid or maid of honor against her will is not going to be a happy camper from the engagement party to the reception. She is going to be the attendant who doesn't return phone calls, misses deadlines, and just doesn't seem to have her heart into being in your wedding. You really ought to commend your friend for knowing ahead of time that being in your wedding would be less of a pleasure and more of a hardship (whether it's a financial, psychological, or emotional hardship).

Now what about the logistics of the bridal party. Will your wedding party be lopsided without this bridesmaid in attendance? Or is this actually a good thing that she canceled on you, because you had too many attendants to begin with? If it does leave your wedding party off balance, and this is something you don't want, you can always "promote" a friend to be a bridesmaid.

So, who do you choose? Do you have any friends of siblings whom you wanted to include in your wedding party but couldn't? Are any of your friends or relatives doing a reading, singing a song, or manning the guest book at your ceremony but would be honored to become a bridesmaid instead? Think about the people to whom you'd already given special jobs to at the wedding as a way of honoring them and see if any one of them might make the perfect bridesmaid candidate. Then make your decisions accordingly.

Q: My pregnant attendant gave birth earlier than expected. Instead of standing up with us at the wedding ceremony, she's in the hospital with her newborn. Now my wedding party is uneven. What should I do?

A: There are certain details about weddings that brides tend to obsess over, such as the color of the flowers, how the pews are decorated, and the organization of their bridal party. But guests at the wedding aren't even aware of these details. Did you know that if you ordered white lilies for your ceremony but you got tiger lilies instead, you would be disappointed but everyone in the audience would think that you chose those lovely orange flowers on purpose? There are some things that you have no control over and can't change, and a baby being born is one of the happier unexpected things that could happen. So why don't you call your new-mom attendant and congratulate her on the birth of her child, and then just go ahead with the wedding, one attendant short? No one will know about her unexpected absence except for you and your other attendants. And really, in the long run, having an uneven wedding party really isn't the worst thing in the world.

Wedding Wisdom

One of my bridesmaids ended up having an emergency C-section and delivered a premature little girl four days before the wedding. She wasn't supposed to deliver until a month later. Lucky for me, another good friend, who wasn't going to be a bridesmaid because she was pregnant, ended up fitting into the new mommy's dress and was able to stand up as a replacement bridesmaid to take her place in the ceremony. She saved the day.
—Emily, Ohio

Q: At every prewedding get-together and event, my bridesmaids and maid of honor fight like cats and dogs. Why can't they all just get along?

A: Have you managed to stock your wedding party with type A, control freaks who always have to get their way? Or did you forget about the long-standing feud between bridesmaids One and Three or how the maid of honor never forgave one of your bridesmaids for dating her now husband when in college? While one would expect adults in a wedding party to act like, well, adults, sometimes that just doesn't happen. So you've got to be the adult in the situation and lay things on the line. Tell your attendants that you're sick of their fighting and that what you really need them to do is to put any of their differences aside for your sake and to be your support system throughout the wedding. Got divorced parents? Then you should be an old pro at navigating between people who can't get along. As long as you tell people up front what you expect of them—namely, their best behavior for your sake—they should rise to the occasion.

Now if you're simply worried that your attendants might fight like cats and dogs, be very careful about whom you choose to be in your wedding party. If you have friends with differences and sisters who will be there for you, no matter what, then this is a situation where the old adage of blood is thicker than water really does apply. Your friends may not be able to put aside their differences—and in reality friends come and go—but your sisters or cousins or other female relatives will always be in your life and be there for you. When in doubt, choose family members to be in your wedding. Or to simplify your life, especially if there are feuding factions to choose from, select one attendant only. That is, you choose a maid of honor and your future husband chooses a best man only. By having only two attendants to deal with, you're sure to avoid the arguments that often occur with larger wedding parties.

Q: I'm no longer friends with one of my attendants and want to "fire" her.

A: Are you truly no longer friends or are you simply so busy with your wedding plans that you haven't been able to hang out with this friend as much and, therefore, feel as if your friendship has waned? If so, then I wouldn't sweat it and just assure your friend that you'll have more time for her once the wedding is over. Why complicate things by asking her to leave the wedding party, just because you're not hanging out all the time anymore?

Now maybe you've had a real falling-out, and you're simply uncomfortable being in the same room with this woman anymore. Well, then, you have two options. You can sit down, try to talk things out with this gal, and figure out how your friendship got off course. Maybe by taking the time to talk, you can patch things up. Of course, this isn't a perfect world, and sometimes friendships have to just run their course—and maybe you just have to accept that, in this case, the friendship has come to the end in the middle of your wedding plans. I don't think it's such a bad idea to be honest with this person and tell her straight out that you think it would be best for all those involved if she didn't continue in her role as bridesmaid. My guess is if you're not really fond of her, she's probably not very fond of you either and would love to have an easy out from your wedding. But you'll never know unless you talk to her. So schedule a time to chat and see how things go from there.

Q: One of my friends won't speak to me because I didn't ask her to be in my wedding.

A: I'm sorry that this is happening to you. The last thing a stressed-out, bride-to-be needs to worry about is mending friendships while she's planning her wedding. Probably the best thing that you can do is take some of the pressure off yourself. How? It's not your fault how your friend reacted to the news that you couldn't include her in your wedding, and you can't control the fact that she doesn't want to speak to you.

If this friend had been expecting to be in your wedding—possibly because you grew up together and always swore that you'd be each other's maid of honor, only she isn't—then it's understandable that her feelings were hurt when you informed her that she wouldn't be a part of your wedding party. But despite hurting her feelings, you shouldn't reward her childish behavior by extending your bridal party or creating a job for her, just to make her happy. Instead, why don't you write her a quick note (handwritten, please) to tell her that you're sorry that her feelings were hurt and that she was disappointed that you couldn't include her in your wedding. Then let her know that you still care for her and hope that you can continue to be friends. If you never hear from her again, then take some comfort in knowing that you've at least done the right thing by reaching out to her and that friendships do ebb and flow. Perhaps it was time for you and this friend to go your separate ways.

Now if you're still in the process of choosing attendants—and there are other friends who might assume they're going to be in your wedding as this girlfriend did, but you can't include them—then act proactively. Let them know ahead of time, either with a phone call, handwritten note, or a chat over a cup of coffee, that while you would really like to include them in your wedding, space, money, or family obligations (whatever your reasons may be) prevent you from doing so. But let these friends know that you knew they might be hurt or taken aback by not being asked to be in the wedding and that's why you wanted to let them know ahead of time. I'm confident that by telling these additional friends the bad news up front, you'll avoid conflicts down the road. And if someone does react like a prima donna, despite your warning her ahead of time, then you should probably reassess that person as a friend anyway. No true friend would put her feelings first when it comes to a good friend's wedding.

Q: The flower girl "quit" our wedding. Now what?

A: Did the flower girl's mother or father explain why their daughter wanted out of your wedding? Was it because she was too afraid to walk down the aisle by herself? I believe that only precocious, outgoing little girls and boys should be asked to be in a wedding. They're the kind of kids who will happily walk or skip down the aisle, much to the delight of the family and friends in the audience. Painfully shy little tykes? I think they could be a recipe for a wedding disaster.

So was your flower girl a bit freaked out by her impending duties? By any chance is her mother in your wedding as well? If so, maybe you could tweak your processional a bit to have her mother walk down the aisle with her daughter, the flower girl, so she won't feel so all alone. If her mother isn't in the wedding but a big sister or favorite aunt is, maybe she could accompany her instead. If that's not possible, then let the poor kid off the hook and figure out Plan B.

Plan B could be that you go entirely without a flower girl—many beautiful weddings have occurred without them—or you could recruit a more outgoing girl for the job. Just make sure that if you do find a stand-in flower girl, you confirm with her parents that she has the perfect personality for the job. You also want a kid with some experience taking direction, such as at a dance recital—you don't want the little sweetheart throwing a temper tantrum halfway down the aisle because she doesn't feel like walking the whole way. You also should confirm that this girl has been in front of large groups before, such as in a church choir or a school's holiday concert. Weddings aren't the best time to have a first bout of stage fright. (But just in case of the temper tantrum or the stage fright, be sure to seat her parents near the front. That way, in a pinch they can come to her rescue.)

Wedding Wisdom

We had three flower girls in our wedding—my niece who was eight years old and my husband's two nieces who were ages two and five at the time. When it came time to walk down the aisle, the first two flower girls went fine, but the youngest didn't want to walk down the aisle. She looked at me and said "Aunt Laurie, I don't want to walk down there." She was so adorable in her little dress and was on the verge of tears. She has these big brown eyes and I was the only person she knew. So...I put her on my left side, my dad was on my right and off we went. We'll always have a special bond because she walked me down the aisle!
—Laurie, Pennsylvania

Q: My nephew is adorable and would be perfect as my ring bearer, but his mom thinks he'll be too afraid to be in my wedding.

A: In a case like this, mother may know best. That is, she knows her son and his quirks. If being in a room with a bunch of strangers looking at him as he carries your wedding bands is likely to cause a crying spell or him to feel paralyzing fear, then you're better off not using this adorable little guy as your ring bearer.

You should use the following criteria and ask these questions of the parents when choosing a ring bearer or any other young child who is going to be a part of your wedding:

- Does this child have an outgoing personality?
- Has this child ever been in front of a large group of people before, such as at a dance recital, church service, or school concert?
- Does this child know how to take direction— and take it well?
- Will this child's parent or parents be in the wedding, just in case he or she needs a familiar face to stand by during the ceremony or in the receiving line?
- Most importantly, is the child genuinely excited about being in your wedding?

The last question really is the most important, because you don't want to force a child, no matter how adorable, to do something that will make him or her miserable. Most children revel in the idea of dressing up and being the center of attention, as they'll likely be as the flower girl or ring bearer in your wedding. But there are some painfully shy children where the same situation that pumps other kids up scares them half to death. Be sure that any young person you choose to be in your wedding feels good about the experience. If you have your doubts—or the parents do—go with someone else. Everyone involved will end up happier in the long run.

Q: Our best man and maid of honor are husband and wife—or at least they were until yesterday—they announced that they were splitting up. Now they don't want to have to see each other at our wedding.

A: It's too bad that your friends' relationship is ending, but having been through parents who divorced and watched friends whose relationships dissolved, here's what I know: I'm pretty sure that this couple knew that their relationship was on the rocks when you asked them to be in your wedding, and they should have said something right then and there. Marriages don't dissolve in a day but over time, so it's too bad that they didn't speak up.

But knowing what they should have done then doesn't help you with your problem now—how to handle having warring factions act civilly during your wedding. First off, tell both your maid of honor and best man that while you're sorry that they'll no longer be together, they each committed to being in your wedding, and you hope that they will follow through with their commitment. If they don't want to, they should tell you now so you can make alternate arrangements. (And do give them this out—it may make things simpler in the end to remove the soon-to-be-divorced couple from the wedding-party equation.) However, if they don't speak up, tell them straight out that you expect them to behave like the adults that they are on your big day—the same sort of stuff you'd tell divorced parents who have the potential not to get along at your wedding. Tell them that you expect them to behave in a civil manner toward one another, not to bad mouth one another while speaking to friends or family, and to participate in all of the traditional things that are expected of best men and maids of honor. Repeat that if they don't think that they can follow through as you're asking them to do, you would appreciate it if they'd step aside now as best man and maid of honor and that way they can just be "regular" guests at your wedding instead.

If for some reason you give them all of their outs and they keep their duties—then behave badly on the big day—try to remain Zen-minded about the whole thing. You can't control how these people are going to act, and if they behave immaturely and like idiots, it is no reflection on you, the bride, but rather on them, the people acting like idiots. Just try to ignore whatever it is they're doing and go on to have a happy wedding day.

Q: The best man "quit" the wedding. Now there's no one to stand up for my fiancé.

A: Does your fiancé have a brother or other family member who could step in for the best man? Did you know that at many of today's modern weddings, couples have opposite sex attendants? That means that if your fiancé has no brothers but does have sisters, maybe one of them could be his best woman.

If a sibling can't step in, is there someone in the wedding party that you could "promote" from usher to best man? Or what about your fiancé's father? I've been to a number of weddings where the groom's father is the best man—and on purpose. So in a worst-case scenario, dear old dad may simply be the best choice for best man.

Q: One of the groomsmen had a fight with my fiancé and now my fiancé doesn't want him to be in the wedding.

A: I'm sure tensions are running high with your wedding plans—that's completely normal. Unfortunately, sometimes things get so tense that folks fight. What exactly did your fiancé fight about with this friend? Are we talking a friendship-ending argument or just a disagreement that got blown out of proportion? Can you step in and try to help mediate things? You may want to gently suggest that your fiancé try to patch things up so your wedding day can go on without any tension between friends. However, if he's resistant to the idea, then back off and let him know that you'll support him in whatever decision he makes about either keeping his friend in the wedding or asking him to leave. And do support him, regardless. Hopefully, the whole thing will blow over, and you won't be left with a lopsided wedding party. But if this argument was the proverbial straw of hay that broke this friendship's back, then take comfort in knowing that it's really no big deal in the long run. If you end up minus an usher at your wedding—and choose not to have someone replace the fired guy—it's not like the wedding etiquette police will descend on your affair because you have more maids than groomsmen. You may just have to reassign things a bit and have two bridesmaids accompany one usher—something I'm sure will be just fine and may even delight your guests for the unique aspect it adds to your wedding ceremony.

Wedding Wisdom

My husband's best friend—and best man—is a very funny guy, and, not surprisingly, the toast he gave at our reception caught everyone's attention, but not for the humorous reasons that I expected. Mike finished his speech by toasting our love as, only Mike could, by calling it 'super-duper-low-cal-melts-in-your-mouth-not-in-your-hand-new-and-improved-energy-efficient-radical-stupendous-tremendus-funky-wonderful.' Only problem was that Mike was so nervous that he said the last part so fast that it sounded like he'd said "f***ing wonderful." Everyone's glasses were held midair and there was this deafening silence. Finally someone in the back of the room started to hesitantly clap and eventually everyone else joined in, very embarrassed and confused. For the rest of the night, I had people coming up to me and asking, "Did the best man actually swear?" I had to repeatedly assure them that our best man did not, in fact ,curse at our reception, but I've never been able to fully convince my grandmother or our priest. I'm just grateful that we opted to forgo a videographer at the reception so I won't have to relive the moment over and over again! I still wince when I think about it!
—Tara, New York

Chapter 7
The Wedding Ceremony

Q: What if there's bad weather on my wedding day?

A: Anyone who plans a special event prays that the weather cooperates—no one wants clouds or rain on a happy occasion. But when it comes right down to it, if there's one thing in life that you can't control, it's the weather. And the sooner you accept the fact, the sooner you'll let go of some of your weather-related stresses for your big day. I'm not saying that you should all dance barefoot in the mud and rain if it storms on your wedding day, but because you can't change whether it will be sunny, snowing, or slushy out, there's no reason to freak out about it.

However, you can plan for rain (or sleet or ice or snow) on your big day in a number of ways.

First, are you planning an outdoor wedding? If so, rent a tent. Even if you live in the driest climate where it never rains, make sure you tent your occasion. Everyone will tell you that you're crazy for doing so, but trust me—you won't regret it. Weddings and weather seem to be ready-made for Murphy's Law. That is, if you don't tent your event, you'll have a freak rainstorm in the middle of your reception, and everyone will get soaked. If you do tent it, the weather will be gorgeous. And if for some reason the weather doesn't cooperate, at least you'll be covered. Literally.

Second, do you have wedding insurance? Believe it or not, policies exist to protect you on your big day. WedSafe, a relatively new company that provides insurance for weddings and other special events, "provides coverage if the weather conditions are extreme enough to prevent the Bride and/or the Groom, their families, or the majority of their guests from attending the wedding or reception," according to its Website *www.wedsafe.com*.

Are you planning a wedding in a place or during a time of the year when weather may usurp your nuptials? Here are some weather-related situations to consider:

- A wedding in Tornado Alley (technically from Texas in the south to Nebraska and Iowa in the north). However, tornadoes can and do happen elsewhere as well. According to the American Meteorology Society's *Glossary of Weather and Climate*, "...although no state is entirely free of tornadoes, they are most frequent in the Plains area between the Rocky Mountains and the Appalachians."
- A winter wedding in an area where snowstorms are common or where there have been damaging ice storms in the past.
- A wedding during hurricane season, which the National Oceanic and Atmospheric Administration (NOAA) defines as occurring between June 1st and November 30th, although hurricanes can happen before or after those official dates. Hurricane season matters if you're planning a celebration on the U.S. mainland or in a destination that is susceptible to both Atlanta and Pacific hurricanes, including Hawaii, Mexico, Bermuda, the Bahamas, and the Caribbean islands.

Wedding Wisdom

I recently was married in an outdoor ceremony that included one uninvited guest—a supercell thunderstorm! The moral of my story is that all brides, no matter what happens, should approach their wedding day with a good sense of humor and a lot of patience. I ended up getting married barefoot and standing in the mud because of the storm that washed away our ceremony site. I handed my shoes and stockings to my mother and asked her to escort my sister (my matron of honor) up the 'aisle' (or what was left of it) and to start the music! My father (soaked tuxedo and all) escorted me, both of us laughing and giggling at the mud between my toes and the rain pouring on our heads. My poor groom and the minister stood there looking like a pair of wet puppies—their hair was clinging to their faces and their clothes were drenched! In the end though, we were married, and my new husband carried me out of the "swamp"—my bare muddy feet dangling for all to see. It was, in short, the most wonderful wedding we could have hoped for!
—Lisa, Louisiana

One Pennsylvania couple who was planning a beachside, September destination wedding in North Carolina wasn't prepared for a weather contingency and paid a steep price for their lack of an alternative plan—they lost thousands of dollars, and had to postpone their wedding and scramble to plan a last-minute wedding back home in the Keystone State.

This couple never considered that a hurricane might come up the coast and affect their wedding. But they should have, given the location of their wedding (Cape Hatteras) and the timing of the wedding (the middle of hurricane season). Unfortunately, Hurricane Isabel was an unexpected guest when she came ashore days before their planned 2003 event and washed away the beach where they were going to tie the knot. This couple had rented a number of beach houses (at great off-season prices) for their guests to stay in during their weekend-long celebration, but unfortunately they paid in cash and lost about $3,000 in the process. (The houses were destroyed.) The only bright spot in their story was their North Carolina-based photographer, who agreed to keep his commitment to the couple and drive to Pennsylvania to photograph their eventual wedding—and at no additional cost.

Had this couple planned ahead or at least insured themselves, they would have realized that planning a fall beachside wedding in North Carolina is a bit risky. (You can check out the NOAA Website at *www.noaa.gov* to track when and where most hurricanes in history have come ashore to see if your chosen spot could conceivably be in the path of a hurricane.)

Third, do you have an alternate plan in place? Find out if the house of worship or the reception site you'll be using has contingency plans for foul weather, loss of power, or anything else weather related that could delay or postpone your wedding. Is there an off-hours phone number you can call the day before the wedding to check in, just in case the weather forecast is looking dicey? The idea here, to borrow from scouting, is to be prepared.

Finally, should the weather not cooperate on your wedding day but not be bad enough to cancel your affair, remember: You cannot control the weather and, regardless of what it is doing outside, you can still have a wonderful wedding day. What matters is that you and your true love will be getting married in front of your friends and loved ones.

Q: I recently moved and discovered that in doing so, I'm no longer considered to be a member of my church's parish because of my new address. I want to be married in my original church but I'm told that I have to use the church that "serves" my new address.

A: Any chance that you still have relatives living within the boundaries of your old parish? Could you change your contact information with the church to one of those addresses to satisfy your church's requirements? Unfortunately, some churches are very strict about who can be married in their church because their parish sizes are so big and they've got to control things in one way or another, so they rely on addresses to do so. I know that where I live, Roman Catholics must follow the rules of the Philadelphia Archdiocese, which is quite serious about assigning people to churches based on their zip code.

They do this because of how fast certain suburban areas are growing and because many parishes simply can't handle the extra families that have moved into the area.

If you are dealing with an inflexible pastor or priest, is it possible for you to take your case to a higher authority, if you will? I would think that if you were a lifelong member of a certain church, they would be foolish to turn you away on your wedding day. Don't give up—keep trying and hopefully the church will change its mind.

If for some reason your old parish won't budge, then you'll have to be married in your "new" church—although there's no guarantee that the other church will be able to honor your original wedding day. So, then you're left with two options: plan a ceremony outside a house of worship, if that's the only way to keep the wedding day that you'd planned for, or change your wedding date so your "new" church can accommodate you.

If you go with the former option, you'll need to come to terms with the fact that that you'll likely have to find a new officiant who may not be affiliated with your faith—and that you may have to find a new place to hold your ceremony. Can your reception locale accommodate you? You may be pleasantly surprised to find out that they can hold both your ceremony and your reception. (They may even be able to recommend an officiant). Or you can call your local town hall to find out if they can suggest a nondenominational officiant, such as the mayor or a local justice of the peace. Although this situation may seem hopeless, it really isn't. You have a number of options available to you that will allow you to still have a great wedding ceremony—even if it occurs in a place you didn't expect.

> ### Wedding Wisdom
>
> A month before the wedding, our priest got transferred to another church a few hours away and he was not permitted to officiate over our service—nor could he attend our reception, due to his new responsibilities. Of course, we were heart broken, because we'd known him for years. But, we quickly worked with the church's new priest to finalize the details, and we went on to have a very beautiful ceremony.
> —Heather, Pennsylvania

Q: We just found out that our house of worship double-booked us. I just assumed that the officiant would be the person I see at worship every week. Now they've booked someone I've never met. I don't want a stranger marrying me.

A: It's probably too late to do anything about the overbooked rabbi or priest who was supposed to lead your wedding ceremony, although I don't think you would be out of line to complain to someone about this mess up. In the meantime ,find a time to meet with the new person. I would think that anyone who is going to marry a couple would want to meet the two people first and have a chance to get to know them. I know that what makes most wedding ceremonies all the more meaningful is when the officiant adds in some personal anecdotes or observations that are unique to the bride and groom. I would hope that your synagogue or church would arrange for you to meet this new rabbi or priest ahead of time.

If the house of worship isn't willing to work with you in this regard, do you have the time or the fortitude to take your wedding ceremony elsewhere? That may be a last-resort option, but if you will truly feel uncomfortable having this stranger marrying you, then finding a new officiant may be your best option. Just make sure that whatever decision you make doesn't cause you anymore stress.

Q: Our church double-booked our wedding date, and said that the only way we could keep our original plans is if we moved our wedding to their smaller chapel. I've got a 14-person wedding party and 200 guests, and there's no way everyone can fit. What are my options?

A: First of all, how close are you to the big day? Have the invitations already been printed and sent? If not, perhaps you can ask your church to be a bit flexible with you and let you hold your ceremony either earlier or later in the day. Given the prospect of completely changing your ceremony date so you can accommodate all of your guests, I would think that a small inconvenience such as moving your ceremony time up or back wouldn't seem to be too much to ask, given that this was the church's mistake to begin with. (They are offering to make good on the goof, right? If not, then you should be bringing this issue up with whoever oversees special events at your house of worship. To inconvenience a couple on their wedding day with a double-booked ceremony simply isn't right!)

If the invitations have already been sent and everything has already been lined up for the ceremony, find out if your house of worship can work with you to take your ceremony outside—this is possibly a stretch but something worth inquiring about.

Also, who's to say that your wedding has to be the one that changes? Sure the house of worship double-booked you, but maybe the other couple has some flexibility in their plans. See if the church can put you in touch with the other couple so you can negotiate about changing the time or date of their wedding. It's possible that they're having a smaller, simpler ceremony, and maybe they can move it to outside or to the smaller chapel.

Finally, if there's simply no flexibility at the church, you may have to forego the church ceremony all together and have your ceremony somewhere else, such as at your reception location.

If you do end up moving the ceremony location at the last minute, put your attendants into crisis mode, and have them start calling all of your guests to let them know of the change. That way, you won't have anyone showing up at the old location and wondering where the heck your wedding has gone.

The most important thing to keep in mind is this: While the news is surely upsetting that everything will not go according to plan, don't let it ruin your wedding plans. Figure out a calm and rational way that you're going to deal with this snafu, and you're sure to come up with a solution, even if it means a compromise on your part.

Q: Our parents are mad because we're not planning to have a religious wedding ceremony. I don't think that they should have a say in how we become husband and wife.

A: Have you considered putting yourself in your parent's shoes for a moment? Perhaps you were raised in a devout Jewish home where you kept kosher, celebrated the Sabbath every Friday night by lighting candles and attending services, and your parents diligently sent you to Hebrew school and had your bat mitzvah on time. Or perhaps your parents raised you as a Roman Catholic and made sure that you received all the sacraments of Catholicism (Baptism, First Holy Communion, and Confirmation) so that you were a full member of your church. Or perhaps you were raised another religion that involved certain time commitments and social sacrifices on your family's behalf so that you, the child, would be raised with a full sense of your faith. Do you have any idea why your parents went through all this trouble? They probably did so for one reason—when it came time for you to marry, you would be able to fully embrace your faith and participate in a religious wedding ceremony within the house of worship where you were raised.

I'm not trying to lecture you on the religious choices and decisions that your parents made to guilt you into doing things their way. Rather, I just wanted to offer up another perspective as to why your parents may be reacting so viscerally to your decision not to have a full Catholic mass at your wedding, to have a justice of the peace marry you instead of the rabbi from your synagogue, or whatever ceremonial idea you may be floating that goes against your religious upbringing. It's very easy to become so self-centered when planning a wedding that it's hard to step outside of yourself and see things from someone else's vantage point. That's all I'm suggesting that you do in regards to your ceremony decision. Then perhaps after having seen things from your parents' perspective, you can open a dialogue with them that will let them express their feelings of disappointment and you can share with them why it is that you've made your decision about your ceremony.

Once you've opened the lines of communication, I hope you, your fiancé, and your parents will be able to discuss openly the reasons behind your ceremony decision—and why you've chosen not to include aspects of your religious upbringing in it.

For example, are you marrying someone of a different faith? If so, then combining two religions in one ceremony and in one house of worship simply may be impossible to pull off. Your parents need to understand that you've already investigated these options—you have, haven't you?—and that you've decided to go the nondenominational route, not out of spite or as a way of thumbing your nose at the establishment but because that's the route that makes the most sense for your wedding.

Maybe you are marrying someone of the same faith but you hold very different opinions of that faith, which is precluding you from being married in that house of worship. Does it make sense for the two of you to sit down and speak with a pastor, rabbi, or some other kind of counselor to talk about your differences in faith? Can you find a happy medium that will allow you to integrate some aspects of your faith into your wedding ceremony? I'm not suggesting this as a way for one party to give in to the other, but think about it this way: Most people get married because one day, down the road, they want to have children. And when children come into the picture, so does the issue of religion. If you can't figure out now, when you're first married, the role that religion will play in your life, then chances are that when you're about to become parents, the same issue will come up again and again. If the two of you can find a common religious ground now, perhaps you can plan a religious ceremony that will make you and your family happy—and you'll have paved the way for clearer communication about religion in the future.

Q: We just phoned our justice of the peace to ask him a question, and it turns out he never booked our date in his calendar. He's happy to send a replacement to officiate at our wedding, or to work with us on a new wedding date. How could he be so irresponsible?

A: Just be glad that you happened to have called him in advance of your wedding. How bummed out would you have been if he didn't show up at all? Anyway, his irresponsibility is inexcusable, and I would be concerned about working with him in the future—either on a rescheduled wedding date or with any replacement he sends. I mean, if you can't rely on the original guy, who's to say anyone he would recommend would be any more responsible.

So what are your options now? Find a new justice of the peace. Ask around to all the people you know who were married recently by a justice of the peace, and see whom they used and whom they would recommend. The best thing that you can do when hiring anyone for your wedding is to use someone who comes highly recommended. Do not just pick someone out of the phone book—unless that person can offer stellar recommendations or happens to have worked with someone you know and whose opinion you respect. Remember: This is the person who is going to pronounce you husband and wife. Make sure you choose someone you can feel good about officiating at your ceremony.

Q: We misjudged the size of our ceremony site. Not only is there not enough room at the altar for our wedding party, but I don't think there will be enough room for all of our guests.

A: The most important calculation for any couple to make before booking a wedding date or booking a ceremony or reception site is to finalize their guest list. I know that when my husband and I were first planning our wedding, we fell in love with a quaint chapel on a nearby college campus for our ceremony and a similarly stunning yacht club for our reception. It was heartbreaking for us to learn that neither location would work for us once we realized we wanted at least 150 people celebrating with us on our big day. We went back and forth for days about whether or not to cut the guest list so we could keep our great locations, but we discovered in the end that what was most important was who would be with us on our wedding day, and not where we would have our ceremony and celebration.

I hope that you won't be faced with a similar challenge as you deal with your too-small ceremony site—that is, having to cut out guests from the celebration so everyone will fit. Before you make that drastic decision, see if you can't get creative with seating arrangements and other things as well. For example, if the altar won't hold your large wedding party, who says they have to stand up there with you anyway? Why not just have the maid of honor and best man standing up with you and the rest of the party can sit down in the front row? If seating is at a premium, can you extend some of the rows with folding chairs so that you can at least get 10 percent more people seated at the ceremony—assuming that doing so won't go against any fire codes? Does the house of worship have some flexibility in its space? I've been in plenty of churches and synagogues that have foldaway walls that reveal additional seating—or at least additional space for seats when crowds go over capacity. Even if you can't seat everyone, maybe you can ask some folks to stand or some other creative measure so you can avoid cutting family and friends from the guest list. Worst-case scenario? You find a new ceremony site at the last minute that will easily accommodate your wedding party and guests.

Q: My officiant is a low talker, and I'm afraid no one will be able to hear him.

A: Is putting a microphone on him an option? See if your videographer was planning on miking everyone for the ceremony—and if he wasn't, perhaps you can convince him to do so, especially in light of your low-talking officiant.

If a microphone won't seem to solve your problem, can you inquire about having another officiant at your house of worship perform your ceremony? Most churches and temples employ at least two spiritual leaders, so I don't think it would be out of line for you to at least inquire about booking a different officiant. I mean, unless you have a personal and long-term relationship with this low-talker, I would think that his inability to speak clearly would be grounds for finding someone else to lead your wedding ceremony.

Finally—and this may seem crazy—but is it possible for you simply not worry about how the officiant sounds? Unless you are having a ceremony that is audience responsive, it shouldn't really matter (although it would be nice) if your guests can hear exactly what the officiant is saying. In fact, in my experience, brides and grooms are so nervous at most weddings that they end up mumbling their lines anyway.

Q: I don't like the officiant at our house of worship.

A: Is this person your only choice? I know that many houses of worship employ at least two spiritual leaders—even if only on a freelance basis—so it would seem to me that you should have some flexibility in the person who leads your service. I know a bride who was very fond of two of the priests at her church but had few nice things to say about a third priest who tended to ad lib at wedding ceremonies and was a real wild card (well, as wild as a priest can be) when he got in front of a congregation. Ask and find out if the day and time you book your wedding will determine which officiant you get—it's possible if you choose another time or date, you'll get someone you like better. That's what this bride did to avoid the ad-libbing officiant, and she found out that he was taking a sabbatical right after the time she wanted to hold her wedding. By pushing her wedding back by two weeks, she was assured that one of the two favored priests would be the ones leading her ceremony.

If changing the time or the date of your wedding ceremony won't fix anything—because this officiant is the only one that your house of worship uses—then you have two options. One, you can live with the officiant and his/her antics and know that your guests won't think any less of your wedding ceremony because of the person who is marrying you. Or, two, you could move your ceremony somewhere else.

If the politics of moving your ceremony to another house of worship seem too difficult, could you find someplace neutral to have your ceremony that won't seem too much of a religious stretch? For example, do you happen to live near the college from where one of you graduated? If so, is there a nondenominational chapel where alumni can hold weddings? Might moving your wedding to such a location make the most sense? One of the places that my husband and I considered holding our wedding ceremony was in the college chapel where my husband's father graduated. It was an ecumenical chapel that would have allowed us to bring in our own officiant for the service. Perhaps this is what you can do as well—especially if you know someone who could lead the ceremony but isn't affiliated with the house of worship where you were originally planning to be married.

Q: The priest at my church won't marry us because we're of differing religions.

A: Many religions have certain restrictions about officiants overseeing a marriage of people of differing religions, and in my experience the more conservative your denomination, the more restrictive religious leaders will be about the services and celebrations they'll officiate at in the house of worship.

So if you were raised in a conservative religion, it shouldn't surprise you that your priest wants you to marry someone of the same religion—it's a way of guaranteeing the continuity of the faith. That said, I don't think that you should have to find a new fiancé just to satisfy the cleric's requirements.

Unless you think you have a good shot at changing your priest's mind (which is probably unlikely), you're going to have to plan to have your wedding ceremony elsewhere—and have it officiated by someone else.

You may have luck planning your wedding at a nondenominational chapel affiliated with a college one of you attended or that is situated near where you live. (Many colleges let non-alums have weddings in their chapels. Friends of ours were married in the chapel at Columbia University although neither was a Columbia grad.) Then you can use the cleric affiliated with that chapel, which, just based on the fact that he or she works on a college campus, is likely to be a bit more flexible about your wedding ceremony and the fact that you guys come from two different religions.

If going the college chapel route doesn't pan out, you may have to go with a completely nondenominational ceremony in a completely nonreligious location, such as in a garden or in your reception locale. You can bring in a justice of the peace to officiate or whomever else you know and like who is able to marry folks. In fact, often the best bet for multireligious couples is to take the ceremony out of a potentially contentious religious setting and go the nondenomination route all together.

Finally, does it make sense for one of you to consider converting? I realize that one's religion can be a sensitive topic for some, but if one of you isn't as devout as the other or doesn't have as strong feelings about their "original" religion, perhaps you might want to discuss the notion of conversion. Of course, converting to a new religion will take time and commitment, so make sure you make this decision well in advance of your wedding day. But if you both end up being the same religion in the end, you'll have solved a big quandary not only for your wedding day, but also for your future when and if you end up having children.

Q: The rabbi at my synagogue has decided he won't marry us because my fiancé's not Jewish. I was planning on having a Jewish wedding with a rabbi present, but now it looks as though that won't happen.

A: There's no reason you can't still have a Jewish wedding—or at least a partially Jewish wedding—even if you don't get married in a synagogue. In fact, you're not alone in wanting to have portions of your own religion woven into your wedding ceremony, even if you're marrying someone who isn't Jewish.

According to statistics, about 50 percent of all weddings involve a Jewish person who is marrying a non-Jew. So you won't be the first Jewish bride to walk down the aisle to your huppah or to sign your Ketubah while also lighting a unity candle to honor your future spouse's non-Jewish roots.

Because so many Jewish people are marrying outside of the faith, fewer and fewer rabbis are willing to officiate at these weddings, which one New England rabbi classified as "detrimental to the future of Jewish life." Don't lose faith, though. There are a number of rabbis and interfaith ministers who are happy to perform your wedding—even with a priest standing by. The trick, of course, is finding the right person.

Type "rabbi to officiate at interfaith wedding" in Google, and you're likely to receive nearly 1,000 hits in return. Sure, many of these hits are rabbis who are posting their disgust at the intermarrying of Jews and the rabbis that officiate at them. But you're also likely to find the personal Websites of rabbis who participate in this veritable cottage industry of performing interfaith Jewish weddings.

One of the pioneers in this area is a man named Rabbi Irwin H. Fishbein, the director of the Rabbinic Center for Research and Counseling in Westfield, New Jersey, a New York City suburb. Rabbi Fishbein has gone through the painstaking process of collecting the names and contact information for approximately 330 rabbis—in the United States and other countries as well—who will officiate at an interfaith wedding. While Argentina and England each have a participating rabbi, and Canada has two (one in Quebec and one in Saskatchewan), the rest reside in the United States. The five states with the greatest concentration of participating rabbis are: California (59), New York (32), Florida (27), Pennsylvania (23), and Ohio (19). (New Jersey comes in at a close sixth with 18 participating rabbis.)

Many of these rabbis have stricter contingencies than others about the kinds of weddings they'll perform. For example, according to Rabbi Fishbein's Website, 59 percent of the rabbis will officiate only if the couple promise to raise their children Jewish, while 45 percent will officiate at a ceremony with other clergy present (the rest won't). Thirteen percent of the rabbis will officiate at a church or chapel with Christian symbols on display, and only a small portion (9 percent) will participate in a ceremony occurring on the Sabbath (sundown Friday to sundown Saturday) or a Jewish holiday.

For a complete compilation of Rabbi Fishbein's list, visit his Website at *www.rcronline.org* or call 908-233-0419. You may be interested to peruse his collection of interfaith Jewish marriage contracts, called a "Ketubah." If you think outside the shul, you're sure to find the right officiant for your interfaith Jewish wedding.

Wedding Wisdom

I'm Jewish, and our tradition is to have my veil cover my face throughout the ceremony. The wedding coordinator suggested that just before my parents gave me away to the groom, they lift my veil, give me a kiss, and put the veil back down for the ceremony. When the time came for my parents to lift my veil, they got so nervous that they basically lifted the veil and headband straight off my head! They both panicked and tried to fix things, but succeeded only in making matters worse, and got all tangled up in my veil. I had to literally pull both their hands off my head, tell them to take a step back, and rearrange the veil myself. They were still so flustered that my mom ended up kissing me somewhere on my head, and I think my dad missed my cheek altogether. Somehow I was able to do all of this while laughing and smiling—and once the veil was in place, we moved on with the ceremony. People actually told me that it was one of their favorite moments of the ceremony, because it was such a real moment. I've even kept it in the video!
—Ilana, New Jersey

Q: My church is always boiling hot. I'm afraid people are going to pass out from the heat.

A: Whether you're having a summer or winter wedding, you can be proactive in dealing with your hotter-than-you-know-what church by giving your guests fans. Yes, I said fans. In fact, handing out pretty paper fans with your programs will add a nice touch to your ceremony. Imagine how pretty it will look with people flipping their fans—like there's a swarm of butterflies that landed at your wedding ceremony. Party supply stores stock paper fans, and I'm sure you could find a stationer or other company that could personalize the fans with your names and wedding date. If you're cash-strapped or confused about what to give as favors, let the fans do double duty. They will be unique and they'll be functional—a great combination that's sure to make your guests happy and comfortable at the same time. Of course, if you don't want to give your guests too many things to juggle, you can rest assured that when the going gets hot, your guests will likely just use their programs as makeshift fans. You may even want to consider printing the programs on your home computer and folding them to look like fans. Punching a hole through the folds can add an elegant touch to a pesky problem.

Q: My synagogue is always freezing cold.

A: Ah, don't you just love climate control? Either you're in a house of worship that's so old and drafty that you freeze in the winter and boil in the summer, or it is so well air-conditioned that even when it's boiling outside, you're freezing inside.

I think a good bet would be to warn your guests ahead of time about the uncertain climate control at your ceremony site so that they can come prepared. I've seen wedding invitations that include a little note about an outdoor wedding where guests would be advised to apply sunblock and wear a hat lest they get burned during the ceremony (little tidbits of information that I, as a guest, always appreciate). So why not include a little note about the freezing cold aspect of your church or synagogue and advise people to bring a wrap, coat, or something else so that they'll be comfortable during the ceremony? Or you can simply make sure that you have a ceremony that moves quickly so no one has to endure the chilly temperatures for too long. And you, the bride, should also keep the temperature thing in mind as you shop for your dress—especially if you're having a winter wedding in a church that's likely to be bitter cold. While you may be tempted to go with a strapless gown because it looks so good, you may do better with a more functional gown that will keep you warm and looks great. Maybe you could find a lovely compromise, such as a strapless gown that comes with a removable bolero jacket that you can wear during the ceremony and then take off at your reception.

Q: My wedding day is the same day that daylight savings changes. I don't want my guests showing up late to my wedding—or arriving an hour early. How can I make sure that everything goes according to plan and on time?

A: You can do what my cousin Cara recently did for her wedding, which occurred on the Sunday that daylight-savings time ended. When she mailed her invitations, she included a note that said, "Remember! Set your clock back one hour. Daylight-savings time ends Sunday, October 26" (the day of her wedding). Cleverly, Cara and her future husband, Jay, had this reminder printed on a color of paper that was different in shape, size, and texture from her invitation, so you couldn't help but see it. That reminder stayed up on my bulletin board with her invitation, and not only did it help me to remember exactly when daylight-savings time ended that year (I can never recall when to fall back or spring forward), but it ensured that my family and the rest of the guests got to the chapel on time.

Q: I visited our wedding ceremony site one Friday evening to meet with the organist, and I couldn't believe how loud the place was. There was so much traffic outside that I could barely hear myself talk. I'm having a Friday night wedding, so does it mean that my ceremony is going to sound like Grand Central Station?

A: Probably, I'm afraid to say. You know how you're supposed to see your reception band in action at someone else's wedding so you can see firsthand how they're likely to behave at your own? Well, the same advice holds true for your ceremony site and your reception location as well. For example, one bride I know booked a lovely country estate for her wedding reception and visited it often on her drive home from work. However, what she never anticipated when booking the place was this: Her county's largest flea market was just down the road from this estate, which meant not only would crossing traffic to get into the estate become impossible on the Saturday of her wedding, but traffic was likely to be backed up for miles, guaranteeing that no one would arrive to her reception on time.

It's critical that you visit both your ceremony and reception site before your big day and at the time of day when your event will be happening. This will clue you into such annoying things as loud traffic during rush hour—maybe you can push your wedding back a few hours to avoid the beep-beep of cars going by—or any other local intrusions that could affect how smoothly your wedding or reception runs. Is there an airport nearby that might have a busy flight pattern on Saturday nights that you never noticed when you visited during the week? Is there a popular flea market or other attraction close to your site that will mean lots of traffic on the weekend of the wedding—but you'd never know it from visiting during the week? You need to plan for all of these contingencies so you don't get caught by mistake.

A good place to start your plan is by asking those who work at and those who've had weddings or receptions at the locales you're planning to use. Find out if there were any things that caught them by surprise, such as low-flying aircraft or a boiling-hot cocktail hour because the sun had whipped around the building and was now baking everyone inside. You could get lucky and find out that the pesky rush hour traffic is the only thing you have to deal with—and perhaps you'll have been lucky enough to plan your affair on a holiday weekend, when everyone will be leaving work earlier than expected, thus leaving your house of worship as quiet and as peaceful as you imagined it would be. But don't leave things like noise pollution to chance—find out ahead of time so that when your officiant asks if you take this man as your lawfully wedded husband, you don't reply by yelling, "What?"

Of course, if you find yourself unable to control the traffic or the noise level at the ceremony, at least you can do something to overcome it. And that is to plan ahead to have access to microphones for everyone who will be speaking, singing or playing music at the ceremony. That way if you can't beat the noise outside, at least you'll be making an attempt to overcome it by making sure everyone at your wedding ceremony can hear your "I do's."

Wedding Wisdom

We planned to have an outdoor, garden ceremony at our reception site—even though we knew we were risking things with the weather. Luckily, the wedding coordinator who worked with the reception site promised she could set up an alternate ceremony site inside, should the weather turn nasty. Twenty minutes before the ceremony, with grey clouds looming, we decided to risk things and start the outdoor ceremony. The rain held off until after the reception began and we were safely inside.
—Cara, New York

Q: I'm afraid the huppah is going to collapse during our wedding ceremony.

A: Well, it just might. Let me recite a passage from my third book *Your Wedding Your Way* (Contemporary Books, 2000) about what role the huppah plays in a Jewish wedding ceremony:

"In Jewish ceremonies the bride and groom are married underneath a huppah, or a bridal canopy, which is a piece of cloth held aloft by four poles. The huppah symbolizes the home the bride and the groom will make together after they are married. Supposedly, the huppah is not a sturdy contraption—it could collapse at any time—in order to show how fragile a marriage between two people can be if they are not careful. The symbolism here is wonderful."

That said, you would be smart to ask four strong and steady people to hold the huppah during your ceremony. While it may wobble from time to time, as long as you have four sturdy sets of hands holding up your huppah, you shouldn't have to worry about it collapsing on you.

Q: My husband cut his foot while breaking the glass after the ceremony. Now the paramedics are here and bandaging his foot.

A: There are two precautions that couples going to break the glass at the ceremony should make. One, they should practice stepping on a glass so they'll know how much (or little) force they need to turn this drinking object into shards. And second, they should be sure to wear footwear that won't fall apart upon breaking the glass, which is what it sounds like happened with your husband.

I'm sorry to hear about his injury, and I hope someone can run out and get him a pair of crutches (if the paramedics don't have a pair) so he can hobble his way through the rest of your wedding celebration.

For couples who are afraid of how real glass might cut a foot, why not call a prop house if there happens to be one located near you (probably not a stretch in movie-making cities such as New York, Los Angeles, and Toronto)? They supply movie directors with fake glass that breaks and sounds like real glass for stunts, but which won't leave actors cut to shreds. Maybe they could supply you with a fake glass cup so that the glass-breaking element of your ceremony looks and sounds real, but leaves little risk involved.

Wedding Wisdom

A week before my wedding I found my ceremony site under construction. We're not talking a few cones and such—the entire site had been ripped up. Our event company had neglected to pull the permit for our public park ceremony site and so we were never told about the construction project. We'd searched for six months for an affordable ceremony site that had a mountain view, something you would think would be easier to find in Colorado. A week before the wedding was not enough time to look for another location with a mountain view. After a few hours of deliberations and negotiations with the event company, we decided our only option was to hold the ceremony in the reception site's gardens, which did not have a mountain view. But 'gardens' isn't exactly the right word. We were in the middle of a drought, and the area had not been planted yet. It was just mounds of dirt. To mitigate the bareness of the site, we negotiated that the event company would pay for a large tent with cocktail tables and linens, and extra served hors d'oeuvre. We had them set up for our musicians and a sound system tent, an extra hors d'oeuvre display at the reception site, plus pay for a full bar. This company ended up paying thousands of dollars in concessions for their mistake of not pulling a $150 permit. After more phone calls, pleading and pressuring, the gardens were planted, with (albeit very small) plants 48 hours before! Despite all of the hassle, on the wedding day, the weather was perfect and the site—with rose bushes blooming, trees flowering, the small plants planted and the white tents—was gorgeous.
—Rebecca, Colorado

Chapter 8
The Entertainment

Q: How do I avoid having bad music/performers at my wedding ceremony and/or reception? I'm so worried that the people I hire are going to stink.

A: Before I answer that question, answer me this: Whom did you hire to perform at your wedding ceremony? And does this musician have a proven track record of doing a good job at weddings? If you can't answer the last question in the affirmative, then you need to find another soloist or string quartet or whomever it is you thought would play at your wedding. Let's go through all of your potential options—and probable solutions—for avoiding bad music at your wedding ceremony and at your reception:

- **Your house of worship offers an organist/soloist.**

  Having entertainment that comes free with your ceremony locale seems like a great deal for the couple that's watching their purse strings. But don't let your wallet do all the talking just yet. Unless you've been to a wedding at this house of worship or have experienced this soloist, organist, or performer first hand, I wouldn't risk taking this church/synagogue up on their offer of a performer just because it's free. However, that doesn't mean that you shouldn't check this person out ahead of time. For all you know he/she could be an amazing organist or vocalist, and the reason the house of worship encourages you to use him/her isn't because of some shady, under-the-table dealings, but simply because they're being altruistic. So see if and when the recommended performer will be doing his or her thing at this house of worship, and sit in on the performance.

You may be pleasantly surprised. However, if he or she turns out to be incredibly awful, especially *if* there is a fee to use him or her, then you will have made an educated decision not to hire the person to perform at your wedding. You must then speak with the officiant about using someone else for your wedding music. Don't be surprised if the house of worship won't negotiate with you on this matter—many churches and synagogues have strict rules about how weddings run, and it could be their way with musicians or the highway. If it comes down to it—and the musician is really that awful— you may need to find an alternative place to tie the knot or see if you can't convince your house of worship to let you substitute electronic music (that is, a CD player) for the real thing.

- **You have a friend/relative who fancies herself a performer.**

    When a friend of ours got married many years ago, she had her friend sing a number of songs in the ceremony. Some thought she was risking things by asking an amateur to take the job of vocalist. But what these naysayers didn't realize was this friend has been the lead singer in most of her high school plays and was currently pursuing a career on Broadway. Granted, not all of your friends or relatives may be Broadway bound, but if you have a friend or family member who has extensive experience performing in front of audiences and you find her singing or music-playing ability quite good, then I would strongly recommend using this friend in your wedding ceremony. However, if you have a friend or family member who would like to use performing at your wedding as a resume builder or as a way to get more experience—but he or she doesn't have tremendous prior experience performing—then you should politely decline his or her offer to perform at the wedding.

- **There's a music department at a nearby college where you can find musicians for a small fee.**

    In theory, this is an awesome idea—tap into the local music department and find students to inexpensively play at your wedding ceremony or even your reception. The problem is that while the musicians may be inexpensive, they may be inexperienced as well. I'm not saying that your local college doesn't breed talented musicians, but weddings are a unique performance situation. Unless you're working with someone who understands the timing issues involved with a wedding—such as the processional and the recessional—you may find yourself walking down the aisle to a recessional that's already ended, or, worse off, to the wrong piece of music. So go ahead and tap into that local music department to save money, but only do so if the department can offer performers who have experience with weddings—and can provide the references to prove it. Then make sure that you schedule a few meetings with these students—including a musical audition—so you feel confident that the students will do a good job. Remember: If they're nervous playing in front of you, imagine how they'll behave in front of an entire congregation? Keep this notion in mind as you figure out whether or not it's worth it to save money by hiring student musicians.

Your mother insists that you use the string quartet that all of her girlfriends' daughters have used at their weddings.

It's wonderful when you can hire a musician (or any other vendor) that someone you know has used at their wedding. But were the people pleased with the performance? Or had they chosen this quartet simply because that's the music everyone in their social circle chooses? When I was a young single thing in New York City, everyone I knew who was someone (or thought they were someone) insisted that they must have this one bandleader perform at their wedding reception. Never mind that the guy was, like, 100 years old and impossible to deal with. If you wanted to make the right impression at your wedding, you hired him. In my opinion, that's a stupid reason to use a certain vendor, and I hope you won't let your parents' (or your own) social stigma get in the way of your making a smart business decision—especially if you're not fond of these musicians or haven't heard good things about them. It may be best to explain this to your mother.

However, if they're fabulous musicians, they fit your budget, and they're available, why not use them? I know brides often want to mark their territory, if you will, when it comes to wedding planning by having a say in every single decision. But maybe in this instance mother and father do know best. So unless you had an alternate plan, why not chill out about the musicians and go with the ones your mom suggests?

※ **Your reception site has a "recommended" list of bandleaders and deejays—none of which you've heard good things about.**

While it can be a wonderful thing to have a ceremony or reception site refer you to musicians and other vendors, when that referral becomes a quid pro quo—you book a certain site, you have to use their "recommended" vendor—that's a red flag in my book. I believe a bride and groom should be free to choose any vendor they feel will work best for their wedding. If a ceremony or reception site wants to put the kibosh on that freedom, then you should be free to take your business elsewhere. But before you walk out on the deal, give their vendors a shot. Arrange to see this band or deejay in action, then ask for at least three references from couples who used them recently. If the site stonewalls you or refuses to cooperate in arranging a viewing or sending you referrals, that's more red flags, and not only should you find different entertainers, you should find a completely different site to use as well.

By keeping these ideas in mind, you're sure to hire musicians for your wedding ceremony and reception who don't stink.

Q: The band we'd hired for the reception just announced they're breaking up. I think it's too late to find another band.

A: Any chance that members of Band A, the original band, may be forming a new band, we'll be calling Band B? And any chance that Band B might be available for your wedding? Before you freak out, ask about this possibility. If that doesn't work out, see if Band A can recommend any other bands who offer a similar sound and feel. Then ask for band recommendations from recently married people you know.

Perhaps your reception site can help you find an alternate band as well. Sure, you'll have to start from square one and go through hiring an entirely new vendor, but unless you're going to use a CD player on shuffle as your entertainment—a very viable option, no less, and one that I used at my own wedding reception, but which may not be right for you—you need to do more research to find the right entertainment for your affair.

Q: We called our bandleader to ask him a question and he never booked our date. Now he's not available and he's sending a combo of his I've never heard perform.

A: Is there something in your original contract with him that says he can send a replacement band at any time and for any reason? If so, then he's simply holding up his end of the bargain, although a bit underhandedly—and you need to make sure you read your vendor contracts more carefully in the future.

Poor contract reading skills aside, you need to understand how entertainment companies work. Many of them offer a variety of different bands for different types of parties, not because they want to send you a different combo at the last minute, but rather because they realize that to succeed in the wedding business, they need to offer a band that's right for everyone. So I'm not surprised that this bandleader had another band at his disposal to send at the last minute. But you're right not to want to have to change the sound you imagined for your reception—and the bandleader shouldn't expect you to change your expectations at the last minute.

Make sure you ask plenty of questions of this new band, including the kinds of music they play, how big they are, and all the other inquiries you made when you hired the original band. Most importantly, ensure that you'll be able to see this band in action before your wedding so you'll know, firsthand, whether they'll be able to deliver the kind of entertainment you envision at your wedding. If they can't, see what you can do to get out of your original contract and you'll likely have to start all over again with finding a different kind of entertainment. You may have to forfeit your deposit in changing your mind, even though the band switched on you, but I would think that a decent business owner would offer to refund your deposit if it turns out that he can't deliver the music and the band that he originally promised.

If you find yourself in need of a new band or deejay, you can always visit all-inclusive wedding Websites such as *weddingchannel.com* and then find message boards that are local to your wedding. But keep in mind that when you take advice or suggestions from strangers, such as those you'll find on these boards, you'll have to take everything with a grain of salt. Remember: What someone might call the best band in the world, you may think is the worst band on the planet. So these kinds of sites may be a good starting point if you find yourself in a bind with a band or deejay, but they shouldn't be your "be all, end all" for finding entertainment.

Q: Even though our entertainment is booked for the wedding, I couldn't help but continue to shop around. I found out that a girlfriend of mine paid less for her band than I am paying for mine. Shouldn't I cancel with my original entertainment and go with this better deal?

A: When it comes to hiring the entertainment for your wedding reception, you're definitely dealing with an apples-and-oranges scenario. That is, just because your friend's wedding band cost significantly less than your wedding band, it doesn't mean that her band is significantly better. The same notion applies with a deejay. How do you know that her package will suit your entertainment needs? Here are some things to keep in mind that could affect how much a band or deejay costs, regardless of their quality:

- At what time of the year did your friend's wedding take place? Currently, June and September are the most popular wedding months. This means that wedding vendors can command a premium price for their services during those times. If your friend planned an off-season wedding, such as in March or November, chances are she was able to negotiate a price break with her band.

- On what day of the week was her wedding? Most people want to have a Saturday night affair—and in June or September, no doubt. That makes this the most expensive day of the week to plan a wedding. However, those who go for a Friday afternoon or Sunday morning wedding—and one planned in an off-season month—are likely to have more flexibility in the fees they pay for entertainment (or any other vendor they may hire for their wedding, for that matter).

- How big is her band? A jazz quartet definitely won't cost the same as a 12-piece orchestra. So if you're going for the big-band sound—with a big band, to boot—and your friend preferred light background music with a smaller sound, then she's definitely going to be paying less for her entertainment.

- If she hired a deejay, did he just spin tunes or did he do more than that? Many deejays these days do more than play records. Some arrive at a reception with a cast of characters to entertain your guests, and hand out props to get everyone up and dancing and doing a conga line. Some employ two or three deejays (so you'll never have a lull in your music when one of the deejays takes a break) or even offer a big-screen music video option. Not surprisingly, the more the deejay brings to the party (literally!), the more expensive he's going to be.

- What did she ask her band to do? In other words, how many hours of her reception did she contract to have the band play? And did she also hire the band or portions of the band to play music at her wedding ceremony? Depending on how long the band plays music throughout the affair, and whether or not they're providing extra musical services, that can significantly effect the price you'll pay for entertainment.

- Does she have a connection with the band that could have earned her a discount? One of the smartest things a bride can do when planning a wedding is ask everyone she knows to see if they know someone who works in the wedding business. Why? Because clients who come to a vendor with a personal recommendation can usually get a "friends and family" discount, if you will. If your friend's uncle is the bandleader or this is the same band that everyone in her family uses for weddings, bar mitzvahs, and anniversary parties, then she's likely to be in a unique negotiating position to get the best deal possible.

So before you go breaking your contract with your original entertainment choice, investigate all of these possibilities and see if you're dealing with apples to apples instead of apples to oranges. If her entertainment choice turns out to be a dream come true in all respects, see if you can back out of your original contract and book her amazing entertainment choice. But don't be surprised if you can't—at least without losing your deposit. However, if, including lost deposits, you're still getting a better deal, it may be worth the change in plans.

Q: The band we hired sounded like something you would hear at a high school talent show!

A: Any chance you tried to save money and you did hire a high school band—maybe your younger brother's garage band? The most important thing to keep in mind when hiring the musicians or talent that will entertain your guests at your wedding is this: Be sure to see (and hear) the band or deejay live and in action before you sign on the dotted line. An entertainment company can come with the highest recommendations from couples that have used them in the past, but if these couples have a very different idea of what constitutes a good wedding band—they might want to emulate the headbanger's ball whereas you're going for something a bit more R&B—then those ratings won't mean anything. If you can't see the band at someone else's wedding, then at least view two or three videotapes of their performances at weddings. If you don't like what you see, find another band. (Note: Look and listen closely when viewing the video portfolio of your potential videographers. You may find a terrific entertainment company performing in these videos, and be sure to ask the videographers if he or she can provide contact information for them.)

Q: The bandleader acted completely obnoxious during the reception, yet he seemed so normal when we met him. Can we get our money back?

A: I can't say this piece of advice enough, so I'll just say it again—before you hire the entertainment for your wedding, make sure that you see that bandleader or deejay in action. Someone can seem so completely normal, calm, and just your type when you meet him or her in an office setting, but he or she could take on an entirely different personality in a performance setting. I know one bandleader who is so full of himself on stage (yet so completely polite otherwise) that he's actually shooed people off the dance floor or told people to get out of his way right before one of his solos. Talk about obnoxious. Again, I'm sure this bandleader came with high remarks from the references you checked, but how do you know that these previous couples have the same taste in bandleaders as you do? That's why, once again, make sure you see a live (or videotaped) performance of any entertainment company you're considering, before hiring them. You want to know, firsthand, what to expect when they take the stage.

Q: The bandleader at my girlfriend's wedding spent a great deal of time eating instead of playing music. Now I'm using him at my wedding and I'm worried I'll have to cut him off and get him back to work.

A: When I got married a number of years ago, I designated a cousin and a friend as my go-to people for handling any problems, slipups, or any other unforeseen event that occurred during my wedding reception. When the photographer wasn't sure who to photograph next and was just standing around, my cousin knew to go into action and gently guide her to a group of relatives I knew that I'd wanted photographed. When the caterer seemed to lose track of where there were additional electric outlets, my friend helped her pull up tablecloths and find them. What I'd done was cover myself for any snafus by assigning two people to handle stuff that I surely didn't want to deal with while enjoying my first dance or greeting my guests.

I would recommend that you do the same at your wedding so that when you or your mother notice that the bandleader seems to be spending an extraordinary amount of time eating, or the deejay has made a cozy home for himself at the bar, the designated band liaison or troubleshooter can quickly solve the problem. He or she can remind the culprit that his break is long over and it's time to start the music again. Chances are the bandleader or deejay just lost track of time, and your friend's gentle reminder was all he needed to get back to work.

Speaking of breaks, you need to understand that any vendor you hire to be with you for the duration of your wedding celebration, such as the caterer, photographer, or entertainment, will negotiate break time into the deal. Make sure you look carefully at how much time he or she has allotted for taking breaks and that you're comfortable with their proposed time off. If the bandleader insists on sitting down for 15 minutes every hour, there's going to be a lot of time during a four-hour affair with no music. That seems excessive. Even if the deejay only wants 15 minutes off every two hours, find out what he plans to do about playing music during those breaks. Does he have some CDs he can put on auto play during that time so at least you'll have background music? Does your bandleader show up at every affair with a tape or CD of prerecorded music to play during breaks? Make sure you ask questions such as these before hiring someone to provide entertainment for you.

Finally, check your entertainer's references to ensure his wedding behavior. You want to make sure that he doesn't spend too much time eating when he should be playing music or that he doesn't request so many breaks that you end up with more canned music (during his breaks) than live songs. Also make sure you ask about the drinking habits, if any, of the entertainer.

If you have an open bar—and the entertainer decides to partake of it—you may end up with someone on stage slurring and stumbling through his performance.

Remember: Despite how stellar the music of your entertainer of choice, the last thing you want is silence or prerecorded music at the time when you are looking forward to the father-daughter dance or your guests are suddenly in the mood to hit the dance floor—but the bandleader or deejay is nowhere to be found.

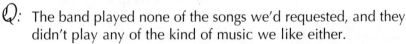

> ## Wedding Wisdom
>
> *Our reception hall lost power in the middle of our party. Our DJ told us to find a battery-powered boom box and play some of our own CDs in it. Because he didn't have any power and couldn't continue spinning tunes, he just left.*
> *—Angela, New York*

Q: The band played none of the songs we'd requested, and they didn't play any of the kind of music we like either.

A: I can't tell you how many times I've heard about brides and grooms who hired an entertainer because they were looking to have a fun reception with all of their favorite dance tunes on the set list. But instead of hip-hop, rhythm and blues, and disco, they got a reception that was more like a hoedown because of the country music the entertainment preferred instead. Or they asked for a specific playlist of songs and barely heard any of the requested tunes.

Talk to bandleaders and deejays about this problem prior to your reception, and they'll tell you that it's impossible to be given a set-in-stone playlist by the couple. They'll tell you that they like to play music based on how the crowd is feeling—dance music to get everyone out onto the dance floor, and then more dance music to keep everyone there—not based on some list that the couple put together. I can appreciate this method to a point—I think that if my deejay had a couple of surefire hits that would get my guests up and boogying, I might be a bit flexible about my suggested playlist, especially if the change in plans resulted in my guests having a great time dancing. But sometimes I think bandleaders and deejays are being prima donnas about their music and want full control over what music they play and when. I'd like to remind these entertainers that the bride and groom are their customers and they are the service providers. If they can't, in good faith, provide the service that the couple wants—whether it's playing a group of requested songs or a specific genre of music—then they should be up front about this discrepancy and suggest the couple take their business elsewhere. I think everyone wins in the end with honesty like this.

That said, I also think it would be in the interest of the couple to realize that bandleaders and deejays have a tremendous amount of experience playing weddings and often really can read a crowd, on the spot, in a way that the couple could never anticipate when they wrote their suggested song list. So here's what I suggest you do.

- When you eventually find the band or deejay service you want to hire for your wedding, let them know up front that there are going to be some specific songs that you want them to play, and that you'd like to create a playlist from which they can work. Also, inform them if there are any kinds of music or specific songs that you don't like and don't want played—and if you can, write this request directly into your service contract. (That way there's a financial disincentive, if you will, for the bandleader or deejay not to ignore your musical preferences.)

- You should also let the bandleader or deejay know that you understand that he or she is a professional and that you respect and appreciate his or her professionalism. Say that you realize that at some point during your reception, if deviating a bit from the suggested playlist may benefit your party by livening things up, you're okay with him or her doing so—as long as he or she doesn't end up playing any of the kinds of music or specific songs that you've pointed out you don't want played at your reception.

- If you know that guests at your wedding aren't going to want really loud music, ask the bandleader or deejay to keep volume in mind. The most common complaint that I hear at wedding receptions is that the music was so loud that people couldn't talk to one another. If you find that the volume seems to have gone up as the night wears on, don't be afraid to ask the band or deejay to tone things down a bit.

Also, you can try to nip the volume problem in the bud by planning your seating charts according to where the band will be set up. That is, place your younger guests closer to the band and their speakers, and your older, more noise-sensitive guests farther away. That way if the band starts to get carried away and the volume starts to creep up, the guest who'll likely enjoy louder music won't mind and your older guests won't be close enough to have the music hurting their ears.

I think that as long as everyone is on the same page about your musical preferences, you're less likely to end up hearing music at your reception that you don't like or didn't expect to hear, and the band or deejay won't disappoint you.

Q: I'm afraid I'm going to forget to tip the deejay/band at the end of the night.

A: I'm sure your entertainment appreciates that you're thinking ahead of time about their tip, and good thing that you are. Chances are, with all that you're going to deal with on your wedding day, you probably will forget to tip them. So take the onus off of yourself for any administrative items you might add to your agenda, such as tipping the waitstaff or the entertainment, and ask someone to do it for you. Arrange in advance to give the tip money to one designated person who won't be busy bidding guests adieu (such as your parents) or gathering your gifts (such as your maid of honor). Instead, find a trustworthy relative or friend who wouldn't mind a special duty at your wedding, and then designate that person as your tipper. Once you've gotten that taken care of, you'll have one less thing to worry about.

Q: I just found out that my deejay is no longer doing weddings. Now we have no one to entertain us at our wedding.

A: First and foremost, did the deejay return your deposit for services he will no longer be rendering? If not, make sure you get your money back. It's not right for the deejay to change his business plans before fulfilling your agreed-upon arrangement—at least without offering to help you find a replacement who can provide a similar service.

Second, unfortunately, you're going to have to start at the beginning again and find another deejay to play at your wedding. Talk to everyone you know who hired a deejay for a recent wedding and see what they had to say about price, performance, and personality. Once you've heard consistently good things about a few deejays, go see them in action—or at least a videotape of them in action. With all this information at your disposal, you're sure to find the perfect replacement deejay.

Q: Our deejay ended up double-booking us. He's trying to make it up to us by sending a friend to play our wedding, but what if his friend is a jerk?

A: I commend your deejay for doing the right thing and suggesting an alternate deejay to entertain at your wedding. However, before you agree to take his replacement, you need to know more about this "friend." Is this really just a friend or a professional associate? Does this person have experience deejaying at weddings? Can this person provide references? Will he cost the same as your original deejay? And, most importantly, will you have the chance to see this person in action beforehand? As long as you get answers to all these questions, and those answers make you feel confident that this guy will do as good a job as your original deejay, then I'd say, yes, definitely take the replacement deejay. But if for some reason you're not convinced, unfortunately you're going to have to begin the search for a new deejay.

Q: The way our deejay behaved at our wedding reception made me feel like we were on a college radio station. He played all sorts of funky tunes and said some pretty nasty stuff into the mike. How come he seemed so normal when we met him?

A: He seemed normal because lots of entertainers and performers have a sort of Dr.-Jekyll-and-Mr.-Hyde thing going on. They're completely normal, even soft-spoken individuals in everyday situations, but put them up on stage or in front of a microphone, and they magically transform into a completely different person. That's why I always advise that when hiring a vendor, not only must you check references for things such as if the vendor shows up on time, but be sure you see that entertainer performing in person (or a reasonable facsimile on videotape). That way you can verify the kind of behavior you can expect to see from this vendor at your wedding reception. This viewing, combined with his references, can help you decide if this is the right entertainer for you. If not, keep looking.

Q: My deejay played the "Chicken Dance" and made my guests do the limbo. I hate all that sort of goofy stuff and thought it spoiled my reception.

A: Yeah, these days whenever you attend a wedding, bar mitzvah, or any other similar event, you can pretty much count on hearing "Hot, Hot, Hot" and the "Chicken Dance" song.

For lots of people, the predictability of this music makes an event more enjoyable. For others, it makes them want to puke.

When you met with your deejay, did you tell him, "No 'Chicken Dance'"? If not, then you can't expect him to read your mind. If there are songs or music genres that you absolutely cannot fathom hearing at your reception, say so up front and let your deejay know, in no uncertain terms, what those offending songs and musical selections are. Unless you speak up, he's never going to know to avoid the neverending conga line that invariably comes together on the dance floor when people hear "Hot, Hot, Hot."

Chapter 9
Photography and Videography

Q: I'm camera shy and don't want to have to go through the whole production of getting my picture taken.

A: If there's one event in your life that everyone expects that you'll capture on film, it's your wedding. And even though you're camera shy, please don't let that preclude you from booking a photographer or videographer. The idea of having your picture taken now may make you feel a bit uncomfortable, but how will you feel in the future? Think about it this way—do you enjoy looking at your baby pictures and other pictures of you as you're growing up? How would you have felt if one of your parents were camera shy and had chosen not to take any pictures of themselves with their kids, including you? Wouldn't you have felt like you were missing something very important in your life?

I urge you to put your photography fears aside and accept the fact that your wedding day is going to involve a lot of photography, and it will be worth it in the long run. Maybe you can speak with your healthcare practitioner about learning some relaxation techniques to overcome your anxiety about having your picture taken. Then you can tap into these techniques if the stress becomes overwhelming on your big day.

Now, given your feelings about being photographed, I would highly recommend that you hire a wedding photographer who specializes in photojournalism. These kinds of photographers capture the essence of an event without being in your guests' faces. The photographer I hired to cover my wedding was just such a photographer, and the biggest compliment our guests gave us after our wedding was that they didn't even know that she was there. Our photographer was so quiet and unassuming in her work that, except for a few flashbulbs here and there, you weren't even aware of her presence. Yet when we saw her photographs of our day, she seemed to have been everywhere and captured everything. It was the best of both worlds.

Should you decide to go the photojournalistic wedding photographer route, don't take these skills for granted. That is, if a photographer's Yellow Pages ad or Website lists "photojournalism," it doesn't mean that he or she is adept at doing it. In fact, photojournalistic has become a major buzzword in wedding photography, so be forewarned. What will really tell you if this photographer knows how to behave photojournalistically is the feedback you get from the references he or she provides (and do get at least three references). You want to hear the kinds of things that my guests said to me about my photographer—"We hardly knew she was there"—and you also want to hear that the photographs that the photographer produced were amazing. I've heard about photojournalistic wedding photographers who were great about staying out of people's way during the wedding, but so much so that the bride and groom didn't feel like the photographer captured the full essence of the wedding. So make sure that any photographer who is commended for being hardly noticeable also produces pictures that the bride and groom find satisfying.

Finally, for the truly photographic-phobic, you can make your picture-taking anxiety easier to deal with if you stick with a still photographer only and forego the videographer. Just make sure you give yourself sufficient time to think about how you may feel in the future if you have no wedding video to watch. Ask your friends who've had wedding videos done how much they watch them and whether they feel it was worth the money and time invested. Then make your decisions accordingly. Who knows, you may be one of the lucky brides who hired a photographer who offers a videography and photography package deal—and has an unobtrusive manner to boot.

Q: Some of the people in my wedding party and my family hate having their picture taken. They're wondering if they can just skip out whenever the photographer or videographer comes near them.

A: For those who are active participants in your wedding, such as your fiancé, your parents, or your attendants, it is pretty imperative that they be a part of the picture-taking process. Talk to them ahead of time about your desire to have them be represented in your pictures, and see if you can't arrange with the photographer to get all of their picture-taking over with in one fell swoop. That way they'll only have to put on their brave face once and for a short period of time, and then they'll know that the pressure will be off of them to look at the camera, smile, and say cheese.

If you have guests who are picture-phobic, there really isn't much you can do about that except to alert your photographer ahead of time that there will be certain people at your wedding who will likely run away when they see the camera coming. If you can, assign someone who knows your guests well to work with the photographer so he or she can direct the photographer away from the folks who find having their picture taken stressful. The last thing you want your guests to feel is as if they're being hounded or chased by a photographer.

Finally, if you come from a photo-phobic family, you would be wise to hire a wedding photographer who specializes in the photojournalistic approach to capture wedding moments. That is, this person excels at completely photographing all aspects of your wedding without being in anyone's face throughout the affair.

Q: My photographer/videographer was a flash in the pan, and now he's gone out of business. Who's going to shoot my wedding?

A: I hope that the vendor at least refunded your deposit before he went out of business, or that you paid for your deposit with a credit card so that you can now dispute the charges.

Financial issues aside, the sad truth is you're going to have to start at the beginning to find another photographer for your wedding. Talk to everyone you know who had a positive experience with a photographer or videographer at a recent wedding, and see if you hear consistently good things about one or two photographers. Then make sure that you meet with each photographer in person before booking him or her.

One of the most important things to keep in mind when hiring a photographer is this: Don't let them show you their "best of" portfolio only—that is, a collection of highlights from a bunch of different weddings that they've photographed. Make sure that you see proofs from a few weddings, from start to finish, so you can get an overall sense of how well the photographer captured everything from the ceremony to the cake-cutting. (This detail is less important with videographers. If anything you want to ask to see the finished product first, because it is the editing of video, along with the shooting of it, that really makes for a great wedding video.) Anyone, even an amateur photographer, can pull off a few good shots, given enough film to work with. But it takes a true professional to capture the unique nuances of a wedding—and capture them well, even in outtakes. If the photographer refuses to show you pictures from the start to finish of a wedding, keep moving—you don't want to work with this person.

Q: We just learned that our original photographer is unable to photograph our wedding—and he was going to provide a videographer as well. He's sending an associate instead, but I've never met this person. Can he do this?

A: You must meet this "associate" before your wedding day and make sure that this associate has as good a portfolio of wedding photographs and/or videos as your original photographer. Keep my basic advice in mind as it refers to hiring a wedding photographer—you only want to work with someone who can show you pictures from a wedding, start to finish, versus a compilation of his best work. Proofs and outtakes from one complete wedding will give you the best overall sense of this photographer's ability. If you like the associate and are happy with his work, then your problem is solved. If you don't and you're unhappy, request your deposit back and find someone else. Unfortunately, that means starting at square one in your search for a wedding photographer, but trust me: You'd rather work with a different wedding photographer who isn't going to flake out or forget to book your wedding date (as your original photographer did).

Q: I just discovered that the local community college has a photography department, including film, and some of the students and faculty do wedding photography and videography. They charge a lot less than the professional I booked and I'm contemplating switching to the cheaper alternative.

A: I would advise switching only if you could be sure that the old adage that "you get what you pay for" doesn't come true. Of course, a student or professor who dabbles in wedding photography is going to cost a lot less than a professional photographer, but can the student or professor make up in quality what you're going to save in dollars and cents, and peace of mind? That's not to say that you can't find a truly talented wedding photographer or videographer at a college, but just make sure that you apply the same standards to this photographer as you would a professional, or any other vendor you might hire for your wedding. These include having:

- Experience photographing weddings.

- References that you can check and which provide good information about this photographer.

- A portfolio of work that includes outtakes and/or proofs that chronicles a wedding from start to finish. (Don't be fooled by a best-of portfolio.) You want to be able to see how well the photographer captures everything from the bride walking down the aisle to the last dance of the evening—and everything in between.

❧ Access to developing, printing, and editing equipment that will ensure a professional-looking wedding album or video in the end.

If the cheaper, college-affiliated photographer or videographer passes all these tests—and you won't be penalized financially for canceling your contract with the original photographer—then by all means go ahead and book this person.

Q: The photographer just called to tell me that he discovered that one of his cameras, including the video camera that his videographer was using, was malfunctioning during my wedding. Then the lab lost some of the film. Now I'm out a bunch of pictures from my event.

A: At least you said that "one of the photographer's cameras" malfunctioned. That tells me that this person arrived at your event with more than one camera and is, in my opinion, the sign of a true professional.

Before you hire any photographer or videographer to shoot your wedding, always ask, "What kind of backup equipment do you bring with you?" I learned this lesson the hard way back in the days when I did freelance event photography. Once, in the middle of an event, my camera stopped advancing. I couldn't take pictures, and I didn't have another camera body with me. So I had to hope that I got enough good shots off to please the client before my camera stopped working (I did, luckily), and I learned that I should never show up as a photographer with only one piece of equipment in hand.

Your photographer should understand that flashes stop working, cameras stop advancing, video cameras go on the fritz, and other sorts of snafus are bound to happen at the worst possible time. That's why professional photographers know that backup equipment is a must. If, when interviewing potential photographers and videographers, you ask them about backup equipment and they look at you quizzically—as if to say that they never heard of such a thing—move on and find another vendor to interview. The last thing you want to do is risk not having photographs of your wedding because some photographer is too cheap to invest in additional equipment or too stupid to realize that it is a necessity.

Now as far as the lost film goes, you really have no control over this, as it's a done deal. But a way to possibly avoid that in the future is to request that your photographer shoot different kinds of film. Ask that he shoot traditional color as well as black and white pictures. Doing so will require that he has at least two camera bodies to work from. You can also request that he shoot large-format film (2 1/4 or 4×5, in photography lingo), which means he'll have to bring yet another kind of camera with him to the wedding. What this helps to do is insure that the different kinds of film will be developed at a different time or a different place, thus giving you some peace of mind that at least one batch (if not all of them) will end up coming back and not getting lost in the process.

Finally, I hope you stocked your reception tables with disposable cameras that your guests can use to photograph their view of your wedding. At least that way, you'll have some photographs of your wedding to put in your album.

Q: I hated working with my photographer/videographer. He was obnoxious to my guests. Can I sue him for pain and suffering?

A: Didn't you check this "professional's" references? Didn't you meet him in person first? I know that many people act differently in an office setting versus at an event, such as a wedding, but I would think that between speaking with other brides and grooms who've contracted him, and speaking with him in person, you would have gotten a good sense of how he would behave at your wedding. I'm sorry to hear that this guy was such an idiot, and maybe you can get compensated for pain and suffering.

I'm talking about the Fair Credit Billing Act (if you paid with a credit card). Since 1974, the Fair Credit Billing Act has protected consumers against unauthorized credit card charges or, in the case of a couple hiring vendors for a wedding, "charges for goods and services [that] weren't delivered as agreed," according to the Federal Trade Commission (FTC) Website at *www.ftc.gov*. (The FTC enforces the Fair Credit

Billing Act.) You may be able to dispute the charge with your credit card company directly or report a violation to the FTC about this obnoxious photographer, thus using the criteria of the Fair Credit Billing Act to sue the unreliable vendor. (You can get the details on how to file a violation on the FTC Website.)

There are a few caveats involving the Fair Credit Billing Act. The first is that the dispute must be for more than $50. Second, the charge in question must have occurred in your home state or within 100 miles of your current billing address. (That means that if you're planning a long-distance wedding, you may not be as successful in disputing charges.) And third, you must have made a good-faith effort first to settle the dispute before bringing in the big guns, such as a lawsuit. (In this instance you're likely to be able to prove a good-faith effort that failed by keeping copies of all correspondence and sending it by certified mail. However, be sure to consult a legal expert if a situation like this arises so you'll feel confident that you've satisfied the notion of a good-faith effort.)

Granted, it's probably easier to dispute a charge on goods or services not delivered, rather than on services delivered in an obnoxious manner. But give it a try—you may just have the law on your side.

Q: My photographer and videographer are friends of the family. They ended up only taking pictures and video of all the people they knew—and none of the other guests at my wedding.

A: It's likely that your friends, the photographer and videographer, fell into the comfort trap and only photographed the people they knew—not a terrible crime, but one that could have easily been avoided. Whether you know the photographer and videographer personally or had a source you trust refer them to you, you should always arm your photographer and videographer with a call sheet (magazines use call sheets when they want to outline their expectations of a photo shoot) for your wedding.

A call sheet for your event would be an outline of what you expect of your photographer and videographer on the day of your wedding. This could include specific people you want to make sure the photographer or videographer captures on film, such as your 96-year-old grandmother, or specific groupings of people. You can put whatever you like on your call sheet. At my wedding reception, I requested that the photographer capture the food presentations (my caterer was out of this world) and the centerpieces on the tables because my mother had made them. I also asked that certain families be photographed together, because my wedding was a mini family reunion for them. Because the photographer had no way of knowing the people I'd referred to on the call sheet, I assigned her an assistant (a cousin of mine) who could bring her around and make sure that she placed the faces to the names on the call sheet. I suggest you do the same. That way, with a call sheet in hand, your photographer and videographer are sure to keep their shooting on track and not focus their cameras on only those they know.

Wedding Wisdom

At the reception, our photographer seemed more interested in flirting with the DJ's assistant than in taking photos. After I asked him twice to keep actively taking photos and then still found him hanging around the DJ stand, I enlisted the help of the banquet hall manager. This particular venue refers a lot of business to the photographer's company, so when she expressed her concerns about his actions, he started snapping away. If I had it to do over again, I would have asked a couple of friends or family members in advance to keep an eye on him and make sure he got shots of everyone.
—Gwen, New Jersey

Q: The photographer handed me 15 rolls of film at the end of the evening and left without saying anything about developing them. Um, I thought that was his job.

A: I think you need to take another look at your photographer's contract (you do have a contract, don't you?) and determine exactly to what services you'd agreed when you hired this photographer. Keep in mind that there are two kinds of wedding photographers. One kind of photographer offers soups-to-nuts packages that include the developing of the film, leather-bound albums, framed pictures, etc. The other kind lets couples choose services on an á la carte basis—basically, you pick and choose what you want the photographer to do, from the most simple—develop photos only—to more elaborate. The difference here, though, is the services don't come as a package deal. Which school of wedding photographer does your guy fit into?

Regardless of which kind of wedding photographer you hired, you need to be clear with the photographer from the start about what your expectations are for your wedding photographs. Then you have to make sure that the services that he offers matches. Is it possible that your photographer wasn't clear about the fact that he works on an á la carte basis? If not, then you should speak with him about what you expected he would cover as your photographer—especially if it seems as though you paid for developing services in advance. If you didn't, then you know that after you return from your honeymoon, your first priority is going to be getting those rolls of film developed and put into an album. Enlargements will, of course, be up to you as well.

Q: We just got our wedding pictures and a rough cut of our wedding video, and everything looks as though an amateur did it. The work I saw in our photographer and videographer's office looked so professional. Did they each send their identical twin "Shaky" instead?

A: You've actually brought up two very important points when it comes to hiring a wedding photographer or videographer. Let me explain.

First, exactly what kinds of examples of his work did he show you when you met with him? Was it a "best of" album, which included amazing pictures from a bunch of different weddings, or great clips from a number of different wedding videos that he shot? If so, then unfortunately your photographer or videographer may have pulled a fast one on you. It's critical that when hiring the person who is going to capture images of your wedding (whether still or video), he shows you previous work that he's done, from start to finish, on at least one or two weddings. Why the start-to-finish requirement? Because it's easy for anyone to pull off a great wedding shot from time to time, thus making great fodder for a "best of" album. But it takes a true professional to capture mostly all, if not all, of a wedding in the best light possible (literally). So if a photographer or videographer can't show you his work from an entire wedding, you should shop elsewhere.

Second, when you met with the photographer or videographer and saw his portfolio of work, was it his own work that you saw? Or was it a collaboration of work done by the various photographers and videographers that this person employs? If you're dealing with an outfit that uses more than one photographer or cameraperson, don't hire someone to shoot your wedding until you can be sure that the person whose work you've seen (and that you like) will be the exact same person who shows up at your wedding. Find out the name of the photographer who seems to do consistently good work, then put that person's name in your contract. That way if his twin brother "Shaky" does show up, you've got great grounds for withholding payment from the photographer. Unfortunately, you'll also have less-than-perfect pictures of your special day, but if you follow my precautions and advice, I'm confident you won't be left with fuzzy or out-of-focus images of your wedding.

Q: My photographer and videographer won't return my calls, and I still haven't seen the photos or video of my wedding?

A: Does the photographer have a place of business that you can visit? If so, then maybe you ought to start showing up there on a regular basis until you can get a straight answer about what happened to your photographs.

If he doesn't have a storefront or office—say he works from his home and met with you at a local coffee shop—than I hope that you at least have his mailing address. Why? Because you need to start sending him letters (via certified or registered mail) that express your displeasure with his behavior. Do you have a lawyer whom you could CC on the letter (even if it's only your brother)? If so, then do that as well. I find that letters that arrive with an attorney CC'd on them tend to get more attention than those arriving without one on it.

If going to these measures does not result in a response, then you'll probably have to bring in an attorney to sue. I just hope that you don't have to get to that point. In the meantime ask all of your guests if they happen to have any photographs from your wedding that they can share with you so that you at least have some photographic record of the day.

Q: The photographer/videographer has decided he wants more money before he'll hand over my wedding photos or video.

A: I may not be a legal expert, but that sounds an awful lot like extortion to me, which is illegal. By any chance, did you pay for his services with a credit card? If so, you may be able to cite the Fair Credit Billing Act of 1974 as way of avoiding paying for his services. (See pages 131-132 for further information.)

So before you hire legal counsel, send this person one or two letters via certified or registered mail that outline the agreement you had originally, including the fee he quoted you and to which you agreed. Include copies of your contract with him as well—you do have a contract, right? If these letters don't work, touch base with a legal expert to find out if what you've done so far satisfies the notion of a good-faith effort. If they do, they you may just have to take this guy to court.

Finally, don't forget to report this unscrupulous photographer/ videographer to your local Better Business Bureau and state's Attorney General's office. These two offices track consumer fraud, and that's exactly what it sounds like this photographer/ videographer is trying to get away with.

Q: The photographer, who is also supplying my videographer, just informed me that there are no accessible electrical outlets at my ceremony location—it's an historical church. So now he says he can't shoot the ceremony. Shouldn't he have checked this first?

A: Actually, I'm happy for you that this photographer had the forethought to check the availability of electricity there— perhaps he has experience photographing weddings in the location and knew to ask first. However, just because there's no electricity doesn't mean that he should automatically write you off as a client. Here are some additional things you should investigate with him:

- If you're getting married during daylight, can he use available light instead of a flash or set-up lights?
- If you're getting married in the evening, is it possible for him to use a film designed for low-light situations, and would adding candles to your ceremony site help in this respect?
- Can he use alternate equipment that doesn't need to be plugged in (battery-powered) to capture your wedding?

The photographer may answer yes to all these additional inquiries, but you need to know if he has experience doing any of these alternatives. Why? Because you don't want a guy who's never shot a wedding by candlelight experimenting with this technique at your wedding. See if he can show you additional images of weddings he's done in similar settings, and then make your final decision based on what you see.

If the photographer wants to back out because he doesn't feel comfortable shooting your wedding under these conditions, then let him go. It's actually a very good sign that he's being up front and honest with you about his capabilities—and that he may be stretching things in a way and won't be able to produce the results you desire.

If you have to let your original photographer go, see if he will refer you to another photographer and videographer who both have more experience dealing with a no-electricity location. Perhaps the historical church where you're getting married can provide recommendations, because it's likely that every couple that marries there deals with this issue when planning a wedding. Once you have the names of a couple of people to check out, make sure you look for pictures that seem to mimic the environment you anticipate at your wedding ceremony—natural light, candlelight, or something similar.

And while I'm sure you'll be stressing out about your unique no-electricity situation, please don't forget the cardinal rule of hiring wedding photographers and videographers: Don't let them show you their "best of" portfolio only—that is, a collection of highlights from a bunch of different weddings that they've photographed. Make sure that you see proofs from a few weddings, from start to finish, or the finished version of a wedding video, so you can get an overall sense of how well the photographer captured everything in the wedding. If the photographer refuses, find another phototgrapher that will.

Q: My dad is an amateur filmmaker and thinks he could do a better job videotaping my wedding. He would be a lot cheaper than the videographer we want to hire. Should I save the bucks and go for it?

A: There are many reasons why I would say no to this idea—and it's not because I have a wedding video company lining my pockets. (I don't, of course.)

First reason to say no: Does your father have any experience taping a wedding? Does he have access to professional paraphernalia, such as a high-definition camera, editing facilities or sound-effects equipment? Your answer to these questions is likely to be no. That means that you may end up with bad footage of your wedding that you'll have to take to a professional in the end to edit. So will you have saved money once it's all said and done? I'm not so sure.

Second reason to say no: Regardless of how tight your wedding budget is, you shouldn't skimp on some things. If having a great looking wedding video is paramount to the two of you, don't let the notion of saving money cloud your judgment. In many things in life, such as with wedding photography, you really do get what you pay for. If dear old dad is going to do this for free, frankly your wedding video is likely to come out looking very much like it was a freebie job.

Third reason to say no: If your dad is busy videotaping the proceedings, how is he going to walk you down the aisle, dance with you, or enjoy his own daughter's wedding? The answer is he's not. He can't do both and he shouldn't try to. Your dad's job, first and foremost, is to be the father of the bride, and that's all he should worry about being or doing on your big day.

Let your father know that you certainly appreciate his offer to videotape your wedding, but tell him that what you want most from him at your wedding is for him to just be dad (not a filmmaker) and for him to be able to enjoy the big day as much as you will. I'm sure your father will appreciate your sentiment.

Chapter 10
The Caterer and Reception

Q: We called our caterer to ask a question and discovered that we hadn't actually been booked for the date we'd agreed upon. Now our date is not available. What can we do?

A: Unless you're willing to change your wedding date—which I wouldn't recommend—then I would find a different caterer and (if the caterer comes with the reception hall) another reception hall. With enough notice given, you should have no problem getting your deposit back.

So now you're back to square one. How can you find a caterer and/or reception hall with a delicious menu, fabulous setting, and superb service?

Start by thinking back to every memorable event you've attended recently. If those events happened to have occurred in the same general vicinity of where you're considering getting married, those locations may be great first places with which to start.

Once you are there, find out if the location has an on-site caterer or contracts with an off-premises caterer. (An off-premises caterer is someone who freelances and cooks at different locations upon request versus an on-site caterer who is booked exclusively through a certain reception location.) In either case, get the name and number of the caterer whose food you've tried firsthand and see if his or her menu options, prices, and availability fit your needs. (If the caterer is the off-premises kind, he or she may even be able to suggest an alternative reception site that you hadn't considered.)

Next, ask all of your friends, family members, and work colleagues who've hosted a wedding or special event recently who they've used for the catering and where they've held their event—and would they recommend either or both as a good and reputable company. Any wedding vendor who comes highly recommended is the one you want to be sure to check out. It's even better if the recommendation comes from someone whose opinion you respect and value.

In addition, be sure you check out the reputation of any caterer, reception hall, or other wedding vendor with your state's Attorney General's office (or the state where the business is located) as well as the Better Business Bureau. You only want to do business with companies that have treated others fairly.

Another great place to check out the good, bad, and ugly of wedding vendors, including caterers and reception halls, is the Internet. If you participate in any wedding-related chat boards, post some questions about that specific vendor or search for any postings about them. Once you find caterer-related postings that are local to your wedding, check out what people have to say about vendors nearby. But always remember that when you take advice or suggestions from strangers, you'll need to do so carefully. What one person deems to be the best cooking on earth, you might call gruel. Similarly, why not do a Google search of the caterer or reception hall? You may come up with some interesting information in the process.

Finally, do not sign on a caterer or reception hall's dotted line until you've tasted their menu. It's not too much for a bride and groom to want to taste ahead of time the kind of menu this caterer or reception hall is going to serve their guests. Try to request that they provide similar items to what they'll present on your wedding day. For example, my wedding reception was a Sunday brunch. So when my husband and I went for a tasting at our caterer's place, they served us zucchini bread and muffins—the very baked goods that we wanted on our menu. By the time we'd finished tasting everything, we knew we'd found the perfect caterer for our affair.

When it comes to hiring the right caterer and/or reception hall, you should follow your heart, your gut, and, of course, your taste buds.

Q: Our caterer double-booked us, and now we have to use an associate we've never met. What if he can't cook?

A: You must meet this "associate" before your wedding day and make sure that this associate is as good a cook as your original caterer. That may mean sitting through a whole other tasting menu with this person (as I'm sure you did with the original caterer) to ensure that this person can make the menu of your dreams. This also means that you should check the references of this new associate just to make sure that he can deliver on the goods (or food, as the case may be) as promised.

If you like the associate and are happy with his cooking, then your problem is solved.

If you're unsatisfied with the cooking or what you hear from other couples who used this alternate caterer, request your deposit back and find someone else. Unfortunately, that may mean starting at square one in your search for a caterer. If this person is the only option you have with your reception hall, then you may have to find another reception hall as well.

Q: I admit it—I'm a bargain shopper who likes to shop around. Even though we booked our caterer, I've found someone cheaper through the local culinary college. Am I stuck or what?

A: Before I can answer that question, I need to know a few things. For starters, what's your commitment with your original caterer? Have you paid for the whole reception up front? Or did you have to pay a deposit only? Would it be cheaper for you in the long run to risk losing the deposit to use this other caterer? In other words, is there a significant difference between the new caterer's overall fee and the deposit? The first caterer is likely not to refund the deposit to you, especially if you've booked him during high wedding season or are canceling at the last minute. However, consider the following to determine your best course of action.

For example, if the first caterer was going to charge you $100 per person and the new caterer will only charge $50 per person, then it may be worth it to risk losing the deposit (which may have been a nominal fee) to save 50 percent overall on your catering bill. However, if you're talking about just a small savings that won't justify breaking your contract with the first caterer, I wouldn't suggest doing it.

Now let's say you're looking at a big savings. That's hard to ignore. But there are other factors to consider when looking at money-saving options—and especially one that involves a college student or someone who doesn't cater weddings for a living.

Unless you're working with someone who understands the timing issues involved with a wedding—such as the cocktail hour or the cake-cutting ceremony—you and your guests may find yourselves with a lull in food service or a missing wedding cake. In addition, you need to make sure that this culinary student has cooked for a large party before (instead of just a small private dinner party) and knows how to staff his or her kitchen so everything for your wedding reception can be made on time. Additionally, if you go with this caterer (instead of your original selection), will you need to rent tables, chairs, linens, and china for your reception—something the original caterer may have handled instead. Finally, can this culinary student provide references whose feedback you find satisfactory? If you have any doubts, go with a professional. But if you happen to stumble upon a culinary student who has experience with all aspects of weddings—and can provide the references to prove it—then it just might make sense to book him or her.

Q: The caterer didn't have the right permits to serve alcohol at our reception location, so now we're having a "dry" wedding. How can I have a champagne toast without the champagne?

A: Sounds like your caterer better stock up on soft drinks and sparkling cider! (By the way, many of my liquor-loving friends often choose to drink sparkling cider over champagne, so don't automatically write off that option, simply because you won't have alcoholic bubbly to serve.)

Now before you declare your wedding reception dry, do a little investigating. I know that in my little town, many restaurants don't want to go through the hassle of securing liquor licenses, so they declare themselves BYO (or Bring Your Own). That allows them to offer customers the option of bringing a bottle of wine to their establishment but doesn't make them responsible for serving it. Can you see if your reception site will let you do something similar? If you supplied the alcohol for your wedding—and placed it on each table, where your guests could serve themselves—would you be able to get around the necessary liquor permits? You may have to do some calling around to the local town clerk's office of the location at which your reception is going to be held to find out about the permits. However, in the process you may uncover some valuable information that will allow you to pop that bottle of bubbly as you celebrate your first dance as husband and wife.

Q: My caterer tells me that he needs to have (but doesn't currently possess) an "open-flame" permit in order to have votive candles on the table and in my centerpieces, and to use Sterno to keep the reception food warm.

A: Unless you plan special events for a living, you've probably never knew there was such a thing as an "open-flame" permit, right? Don't worry—your caterer should be fully familiar with the concept, and he may still have time to get the necessary permits so you can have a reception by candlelight and warm food to feed your guests.

Many towns and cities offer downloadable open-flame permits that have been designed for one-time, special occasions, such as a wedding. While each city has its own rules about the application process, usually you have to go through the police and/or fire department to secure the proper permits. So encourage your caterer to look into this option or you're going to have to change your reception to a location that already has the necessary permits for candles, Sterno, and other flammable objects.

Now if you find that your caterer is completely baffled by the concept of an open flame permit or doesn't seem to know how to go about obtaining one, I'd be leery of his catering abilities. Are you confident you're dealing with a pro? You might want to recheck his references before moving forward on any additional reception plans.

For couples still in the planning process and who are considering having open flames at their wedding, make sure you ask your caterer and/or reception hall about the open flame permit right off the bat. You should know up front whether or not you'll be able to have candles or Sterno in use at your reception—because it will have a big effect on the kind of reception you plan.

Also, if you're planning to have your reception at an historical location, don't be surprised if the open-flame permit option isn't an option. Open-flame permits are designed to prevent fires, and many historical sites that open themselves up for special events don't want to risk having a fire starting on their premises. That's why they don't have an open-flame permit, nor do they allow anyone planning an event at their location to apply for one. I know this to be true because of what happened during my wedding plans.

One of the reception sites my husband and I originally considered for our wedding was the historical society in the town where we grew up. This historical society was situated in a pre-Revolutionary War house, and not only did it have limited electrical outlets, it was a fire-free place. That is, if my caterer wanted to cook or keep food warm during the reception, she was going to have had to do so on portable stoves set up outside and a certain distance away from the structure. Similarly, if I wanted any sort of lighting on our reception tables, I would have had to use battery-operated luminaries (like the kind you put in windows during the holidays) instead of real candles. This place was dead-set on not allowing open-flames on its premises, and even an hysterical bride who had her heart set on candlelight couldn't convince them to change their minds.

So if you really like the idea of having your reception at the local museum or in an historic home, keep my story in mind. You may end up having to choose between a favored location and your desire to have candlelight glowing at your reception.

Wedding Wisdom

I was one of the "Blackout" brides of August 2003. For some reason I'd asked my reception site if they had a backup generator to cover the lighting and all other electrical needs if there was an emergency. When they told us yes, we felt safe booking the place. Who would have known that we would actually end up needing that generator? Well, on the day of the wedding, with the blackout in full force, the reception site's generator went on the fritz. We wanted to light everything with candles, but the fire marshal in town told us that this was a fire hazard and without lights or a working generator, we had to call the whole thing off. Luckily, an uncle of mine owns an emergency environmental company, which uses generators all the time. He got one for the reception site so they could turn the power on and we could have our reception. Unfortunately, by this time most of the food had gone bad and we made do with what we had. Because we'd paid for the reception in advance—and hadn't gotten anything in writing that said we would get a refund if they failed to deliver the services that they'd promised—we didn't get any money back for any of the nonexistent (and now spoiled) menu items that we'd paid for in advance.
—Angela, New York

Q: The caterer used Sterno flames to keep the food warm at the buffet, and it caused a fire. Now the fire department is here and my guests have been evacuated to the parking lot.

A: While I understand that accidents can happen—I've been to events that were interrupted by fire—my guess is your caterer may have hired someone inexperienced in dealing with Sterno to serve food at your wedding. He probably made this hiring decision as a way to save himself overhead—and maybe save you some money on your catering bill—but look what happened instead? He caused a great big headache by practically burning down your reception.

So in hindsight, here's what I suggest: Be sure that when you're interviewing caterers, you query them on where they pull their employee pool from—and how much collective experience their staff has. It's always a good thing when you hear that a caterer or reception hall has employed the same group of people for years running. Staff longevity is a sure sign of a professional operation. On the flip side, though, it may not be such a good sign to hear about high turnover rate on servers or to have the caterer stammer or try to avoid answering the question about where he finds his servers.

In addition to asking the caterer about his service staff, have the caterer provide references of other couples that have used the caterer for a wedding. Ask those couples how the service staff behaved. Might they have had any near misses with out-of-control Sterno that could have resulted in a fire? Did the serving staff seem to know what they were doing? Were they polite to the guests? Would the couple highly recommend the caterer to anyone who asked? Listen carefully to what people say, because there may be some subtle clues that this caterer won't provide the perfect service that he promises.

For example, did one of the reference couples joke about the fact that the service staff didn't seem to know red wine from white wine? While that may seem funny in retrospect, it will make an awful impression on your guests who prefer white wine over red wine, or vice versa. Did the bride and groom complain about how they never saw any food during the entire event? A good caterer with experience working weddings knows that the bride and the groom are usually too busy mingling with guests to sit down and eat. But they need to eat, so a caterer will usually designate someone on his staff to make sure that the bride and the groom have a little nourishment or a glass of water when they need it, or take the time to ensure that the happy couple actually gets to enjoy a slice of their wedding cake. All of the little "aside" comments you may hear while checking references can tell you a lot about how well or how poorly a caterer will serve you and your guests at your reception.

Don't ignore these comments—if anything, listen to them more carefully than anything else. If you come away with a bad feeling about a caterer, find someone else to handle your reception.

Q: We asked our caterer for—and agreed upon—a vegetarian menu. Now they're serving beef to our vegan friends. How could they botch the menu so badly? This isn't what we ordered.

A: One of the most important things that a couple can do to ensure that everything goes as planned on their big day is this: Confirm everything with everyone in writing in the days and weeks prior to the wedding. I always recommend that one to three days before the event, you check back one last time with each of your vendors to make sure everything is still on track. I would call first, and then fax or e-mail a confirmation of what was discussed. That way you can enjoy peace of mind that your vegan friends won't be served beef or that your caterer knows that you want a chocolate wedding cake instead of a vanilla one.

Now let's back up a bit. Say that you're planning a wedding where you'll have, how shall I say it, high-maintenance guests—and I mean that only in the sense that your guests will expect food that departs from the menu one normally expects at a wedding. For example, most caterers know to include a fish of some sort for vegetarian guests to choose from, but all caterers might not be savvy enough to make the distinction between vegetarian and vegan. So, if you know in advance that a majority of your guests will have special dietary needs at your reception—whether they be kosher or vegan—I would recommend booking your wedding reception one of two ways: with either a caterer who specializes in this kind of cooking or food preparation; or at a location where there will be a consultant onsite who can run interference should any menu snafus occur. That way if plates of beef start coming out of the kitchen when the consultant knows they should be plates of stir-fried vegetables, she can stop the waitstaff and get them back on track with the proper dishes.

You want your guests to enjoy the food at your wedding, and you want to make sure they are served something they'll enjoy eating. It would be no fun for non-meat eaters to find a rack of lamb in front of them, nor would the serious carnivore appreciate having a vegetarian meal as his only option. Likewise, if you've got friends or family members with certain diet-related concerns, such as a nut allergy or they must have a gluten-free diet, be sure to ask your caterer about how he or she will accommodate such guests when cooking your menu. For such dietary considerations, you may have to get a little creative. For example, some Whole Foods Markets will bake gluten-free wedding cakes, if either of you has celiac disease or if you want to have a wedding cake that all of your guests (including the gluten-intolerant) can enjoy.

Do your homework on your caterer when you're thinking of planning an offbeat reception menu or a menu that must take dietary needs into consideration, and make sure you feel confident that the caterer will deliver a menu to your guests' (and your own) liking.

Q: My reception hall burned down. Now I have no place to hold the party.

A: Believe it or not, this is exactly what happened to a famed location near where I live. For years couples had been coming from all over the country to be married at this estate. Then one night in the middle of wedding season, there was an electrical fire and the estate was gone. Luckily, the owner of the estate did not live on the premises nor did she keep her business records there. So she escaped from harm and was able to call all of the couples that had weddings booked there in the next month to let them know the bad news. She also offered to help each couple find another place to hold their wedding—even going as far as making phone calls to other (competing) locations nearby to see if they could accommodate her couples. In addition, she did some public relations on behalf of her business's misfortune and was able to get articles in the local paper about her heroic efforts to salvage as many weddings as she could—even though she couldn't personally host any of them in her burned-down location. This publicity generated even more responses from nearby venues, which, together, offered to host each and every wedding that would have otherwise had to have been postponed or cancelled.

Why am I telling you all of this? Because I hope that the person who owns or runs the reception hall where you had hoped to have your reception is doing something similar for you and every other couple who no longer has a reception site for their wedding. If that person isn't, I would suggest calling him or her up and asking if he or she can't help you track down alternate locations for your reception—especially if the fire occurred very close to your big day, putting you in a last-minute bind.

If the owner isn't willing to help out, then you should try to garner some of your own publicity so you can get some help with your wedding situation—and to chronicle your failed attempts to get the reception hall owner to make good on your wedding. I suggest this, not out of spite, but for your own protection. If you have to end up suing the reception hall owner for any money he or she refused to refund or to make a claim on your wedding insurance policy (you do have a wedding insurance policy, don't you?), having articles in a newspaper could help support your claim. Most business owners are decent human beings who would hate to see a wedding day ruined. An article in the paper about your plight could result in a wedding solution you hadn't considered and might allow you to have your wedding as planned, when you planned. Yes, the fire was likely an accident and probably not the fault of the reception hall owner, but there's no reason for him or her not to help out each of the couples that are now inconvenienced because of the fire. Like it or not, this reception hall owner had a business relationship with you, and he or she should do whatever is possible to maintain that relationship with you.

Q: I just read in the newspaper that my reception hall went bankrupt and shut down. Where are we going to have my wedding reception?

A: Obviously you will not hold it in your original location, but you may be able to use that newspaper article to your benefit. Have you considered doing some public relations on behalf of your now-orphaned wedding event? Why not write a letter to the editor of your local paper and tell them about your reaction to their recent article about your reception hall? Your situation could make for a very good story, especially if you're just learning about the reception hall going out of business by reading that newspaper article. Common decency would have you believe that the catering manager at your reception site should have had the courtesy to call you and explain that you'll have to find an alternate place to hold your wedding. Who knows—the paper may decide to do a follow-up story on the couples who were affected by the reception hall's closing, and you could appear in the paper.

Whether the paper prints a letter to the editor or does an article on your behalf, being in the newspaper may help you in the long run. Local business owners could read about you and your situation, and they could get in contact about how they can help you find another location for your wedding. These could be businesses that you wouldn't have thought to contact for help and who may be able to pull strings to help you make last-minute plans. These businesses may be able to offer solutions you hadn't considered that would turn your potential wedding disaster into the perfect wedding day.

Of course, getting your name in the newspaper shouldn't be your only way of solving your problem, although it's a good place to start. You should also strongly suggest that the owner of the original reception hall—if he or she is still around—help you find a new place to have your reception. I'm sure this business owner has contacts in the community who can help. The right thing for the owner to do is to help out any of the inconvenienced couples.

Q: We called our banquet hall manager and discovered that she forgot to enter our wedding date into their database. Now our date is booked up so we can't have our wedding there. What can we do?

A: It sounds like you're going to have to change your wedding venue—or change your wedding date to keep your plans at your original location. Either way, the banquet manager should make good on her mistake.

If you decide to take your wedding reception elsewhere, she should fully refund any money you've given her. If you decide to change your wedding date to accommodate their snafu, she should at least offer to upgrade your menu, provide free premium liquors, or add some other service or amenity free of charge to make up for the fact that you had to change your wedding date. Hopefully, you'll have discovered this mistake long before you've sent out invitations or booked any of your other vendors. If not, your best bet may be to go with a different reception venue so that you can keep all of your other vendors. That way you'll only have one thing to change—reception location. (Remember to inform your vendors as well as your guests of the change.)

If you decide to change your wedding date so you can keep your original reception site, you may have to find new entertainment, photographer, florist, and more because they may all be booked on your alternate date. So figure out what's easiest for you in the long run—although, in my opinion, a change of venue on the same date seems like the simplest solution to the problem.

Q: Even though we booked our reception hall, I just found out that the local fire hall could do our reception for free. Can I change venues at this point?

A: As my husband always says, "Free is our favorite price!" And finding a place at which to hold your wedding for free is something pretty amazing. Before I can help you figure out what to do, let's get some things out in the open.

First, what's your commitment with your original caterer and/or reception hall? Have you paid for the whole reception up front? Or have you given them a deposit only? If you only risk losing a deposit—and you're confident you can have a similar caliber wedding at the fire hall—then changing reception locales may make a lot of sense.

Obviously, you're looking at a huge cost-saving option with the free fire hall—that's hard to beat. But I mentioned something about the caliber of your wedding. Do you know for certain that having your wedding at the fire hall won't affect the kind of wedding you have? That's not to say that you can't have a perfectly wonderful affair at a place such as a fire hall, but if your original location was the conservatory in a botanical garden or the ballroom of a nearby mansion, your wedding is going to take on a completely different feel when your guests arrive at a place where fire engines are parked outside.

So here's what I want you to find out: First and foremost, is the fire hall big enough to accommodate all of the guests you want to invite to your wedding? That's the most important thing for you to determine. If you can answer yes to that question, then find out this additional information:

- What does the fire hall do to transform its banquet room from a stripped-down, oversized space into a place that feels more like where one would celebrate a reception?
- Does the fire hall have special lighting effects, high-end linens, chair covers, and other accoutrements that will give the fire hall more of a ballroom feel?
- What kind of other facilities does the fire hall offer? Is there a full kitchen at the caterer's disposal?

- Does the fire hall have an open flame permit so you can have candles on tables or Sterno to keep food warm?
- Will there be a room for storing coats, gifts, or to put a babysitter to entertain children?
- Can you dress up the restrooms so they don't look like something from a high school?
- What kind of sound system does the hall have?
- Does the system allow you the flexibility to have either a band or a deejay?
- What is the parking situation?

If you can get affirmative answers to all of your questions—and you don't feel like you would be compromising on the caliber of your wedding reception at the fire hall—then by all means, go ahead and book it. It sounds like a great deal. (Keep in mind that, should there be a fire in the area, the alarm will go off, and the noise will be piercing and go on for quite some time during your big day.)

Q: Our families are teetotalers (nondrinkers), yet our friends enjoy cocktails. We don't want to have a dry wedding, which is what our parents are insisting we must do. How can we accommodate both groups?

A: Do you think that your parents will be willing to compromise? Regardless of how old the bride and groom are (unless they're not of legal drinking age, of course) or who is picking up the tab for the wedding, I'm a big believer in the bride and groom having the final say in their wedding decisions. That's not to say that they shouldn't involve their parents in the decision-making process, but they should not hand over all of the decision-making power to their mothers and fathers. Mature couples need to explain, in calm and reasonable terms, that while they appreciate their parents' input in the wedding plans, when it comes down to it, the wedding day is about the couple as much as it is about the families involved. And given that it is the couple's wedding day, most, if not all, of the wedding and reception should be a reflection of the couple.

As far as an alcohol compromise goes, why not suggest that you have a cash bar during the cocktail hour only, instead of an open one? That way there will be more control over who drinks and how much—especially because the alcohol won't be free flowing for the duration of the reception. In addition, you can suggest that your parents and their guests have sparkling cider on the tables at the reception while your friends—the ones who enjoy cocktails—can have bottles of wine on their tables. Not only will this option further limit alcohol consumption, but it can cut down your bar bill considerably—especially if you instruct your caterer or banquet manager to only uncork a bottle of wine upon bringing it to a table. (Negotiate this in advance so that at the end of the night, you only have to pay for the bottles that they opened. This isn't an unreasonable request.)

If, even with your sound negotiating and calm conversations, your parents refuse to consider serving alcohol at their child's wedding, stop for a second and think. Is fighting over something as silly as serving wine at your wedding worth it? Is this really a battle you want to have with your parents before one of the most important days of your life? Relationships are all about choosing battles and making compromises, and you need to decide if avoiding a dry wedding is really worth the effort. Conversely, your parents should probably also decide whether fighting with you over alcohol is worth it, but this a book for brides (not mothers of the brides), so I'm counting on you to figure out a solution to this problem. In the long run, no one will likely remember whether they toasted you with champagne or sparkling cider, so keep that in mind as you make your drink-menu decisions.

Q: We had an open bar at the wedding and, well, let's just say, many people took advantage of the unlimited alcohol. The night ended with everyone too drunk to drive home. Could I have done anything to prevent this?

A: I've met many brides who come from families that enjoy indulging in alcohol or have friends that like to keep their spirits flowing whenever they get together. What these savvy brides knew to do was this: Plan for the worst-case scenario of people being too drunk to drive home. So what did they do? Some had their reception in the same hotel where most of their guests would be staying. That way, when the night was over, the only transportation people would have to take would be the elevator to their room. Others arranged to have trolley buses or vans waiting after the reception to take people home or back to their hotel. Basically, these brides did not want any of their guests to drive drunk so they planned accordingly. If you know that your friends and family are likely to act in a similar way, I suggest you make similar transportation plans.

Wedding Wisdom

I got married when I was 35 and I wanted a beautiful, memorable day without much hassle. I think my age had something to do with this commonsense approach. So when planning our reception, I chose to go with a hotel which provided basically everything. They took care of the flowers, the cake, and the linens for the reception. The honeymoon suite was included, and a discount was provided for the rehearsal dinner and the rooms, and post-wedding day brunch for out-of-town guests. So many details were taken care of in one fell swoop so that planning was a breeze.
—Toni, Pennsylvania

Q: There weren't enough seats for all of my guests to sit down and have dinner. Now people have to stand and eat. Why did this happen?

A: There are a number of reasons that this could have happened—and many ways you could have avoided this situation.

First, were you diligent about collecting RSVPs from your guests? Whether or not your guests replied in a timely manner, it is your responsibility to make sure you get an answer for each and every guest you invited to your wedding. Didn't get their RSVP card? Then you should phone, fax, e-mail, or visit them in person. This way you can give your caterer or banquet manager the most up-to-date head count possible for your reception.

Second, did you confirm your head count with the reception site at least 48 hours before your event? You should always touch base with each of your wedding vendors in the days before your wedding, just to make sure that everything that you discussed and planned for is still in the works. If you don't supply your caterer with an accurate number of guests, there's no way he can plan accordingly for your party size.

Third, are you sure that your reception hall was forthcoming about its capacity? One bride I know found out too late that the restaurant at which she was having her reception couldn't accommodate 200 people—it could only fit enough tables and chairs for 175, so 25 of her guests had to share seats or stand. Her biggest mistake? Not getting the capacity size in writing. Sure, the restaurant owner had verbally assured her that everyone would fit, but afterwards, she had nothing to prove that he'd told her this, and, therefore, she had no recourse in trying to get her money back, as she felt was her right. Learn from her mistake and make sure you get everything in writing—especially when it comes to seating the guests at your reception. Don't end up as this bride did and not know any better, and end up leaving your guests standing up to eat.

Q: I've been to weddings where the bride and groom barely see each other the night of. I don't want to spend my entire wedding reception apart from my groom.

A: I'm sure there are going to be many people that you'll want to see at your wedding reception—and many people that will want to see you as well. But there's no reason for you and your new husband to go in opposite directions, just so you can say hello to everyone before the night is over. Yes, it's nice when the happy couple mingles with their guests, but it's also nice when you can spend time together. That's why I believe that guests should come to the bride and groom's table—not the other way around. So make a plan to sit down at your private table during your wedding reception, and let people come over to see you. Another benefit to sitting down together—you can have something to eat, which may not be your priority when you've got so many people to see and so many dances to dance. You'd be surprised by how people respect a newly married couple when they see them sitting alone together at that table—and especially if they're eating. This way you can sneak in some time together and make sure that you don't end the night in a famished state.

Q: The table holding our wedding cake collapsed at the beginning of the reception. Now we can't do our cake-cutting ceremony and we have nothing to serve for dessert. Help!

A: I thought falling wedding cakes only happened in movies or on television shows. That is until I attended a wedding where the caterer placed the very heavy wedding cake on a very flimsy card table. And just as the bride and the groom were going to cut the cake, the table started to give way. Luckily, the groom was an agile guy and he saved the cake—and the day.

So where does that leave you? Make sure that you discuss, ahead of time, where and how your caterer will display your cake. Express your concerns about collapsing tables and have him or her assure you that the cake will be put someplace safe and sturdy—and not on a card table. If you raise this issue ahead of time, you're likely to avoid having your wedding-cake table collapse on you.

> **Wedding Wisdom**
>
> I neglected to touch base with my reception site the day before my wedding and double-check that everything would be set up as I wanted. So I was unpleasantly surprised to discover that the reception tables had been set up as rounds instead of the long T-shape that I wanted. Only I freaked out because no one else knew what it was supposed to look like, although there is a funny picture of me entering the reception room with a witchy frown and pointing my fingers at the wrong setup.
> —Jillian, Pennsylvania

Q: All of the toasts at the reception were a disaster. First, the best man had an anxiety attack and practically fainted. Then my brother got up and, because he'd had too much to drink, he gave an obscene toast. How could people do this to me?

A: Did you communicate clearly with your designated toast-givers about what you wanted and expected of them with their toasts? And did you give each of the toast-givers the option of backing out, should they feel too nervous or overwhelmed to follow through with their duties? It takes a special kind of person to write and give a toast at a wedding, and I've seen even the most outgoing person become tongue-tied when standing up to deliver a toast. So why not make the lives of your toast-givers a bit easier by doing the following:

1. Only ask people whom you know to be outgoing to give a toast. Standing up in front of hundreds of people—many of whom you do not know—can cause a great deal of anxiety.

2. Give each person you ask to give a toast the option of backing out—with ample warning, of course—in case they have a change of heart.

3. Offer the toast-giver some guidance. Each person giving a toast may play a different role in your

and your future husband's life, so suggest they focus their speech on how they met you, funny stories you would like to share, or even a David Letterman-esque "Top 10" list about you and your husband. To the nonwriter, there's nothing more threatening than a blank piece of paper or a blank computer screen. If you offer some ideas on how they should approach writing their toast, it will make their job much easier.

4. Remember that the toasts people give may be about you, but how they give it is no reflection on you. So if your drunk brother gets up there and starts slurring, be embarrassed for him—not for you. He's an adult and should have known better. Smile and nod as he stumbles through his toast and know, as the old saying goes, this too shall pass.

Q: My mother is forcing me to throw my bouquet. All of my friends are married, so it seems stupid. How should I handle this?

A: Nobody can force you do to anything at your own wedding, so unless your mother is going to literally force your arm into the air and make you release your bouquet, there's no reason for you to fret over tossing your bouquet.

I think that if, indeed, all of your friends are married, it would be a silly thing to do—that is, unless you have a large contingent of little girls at your reception who might get a kick out of participating in the bouquet tossing—or catching, as the case may be. However, if you have many single friends and it might actually be fun to toss your bouquet to one of them, why not take your mother's suggestion? As I said earlier, relationships are all about choosing your battles and making compromises, and you need to think about whether tossing or not tossing your bouquet at your wedding is really a battle that you want to have with your mother. In the long run, who's it going to hurt? Sure, your mother should respect your opinion and not make you do anything that you don't want to do at your wedding. But if you need to save your battles for more important things, go with the bouquet toss. It will save you a lot of grief in the long run.

Q: As is tradition at a Jewish wedding, my guests are going to pick me up in a chair and carry me around the dance floor. I'm afraid of heights, and I'm afraid they're going to drop me. How can I tell them not to do it?

A: I'm not sure you *can* tell them. Having been to many Jewish weddings in my lifetime, I've seen how a dance floor full of people can become so swept up in the emotion of the wedding that, before you know it, there is a bride and groom sitting in chairs and seemingly dancing over the guests' heads. A bride may adamantly refuse to go up in the chairs, but somehow she goes up. People just get carried away and then you have to decide, *Well, do I make a big scene about this whole chair thing or do I just go with it?* I suppose if you don't want to partake of the tradition, you can simply stay away from any chairs that people bring out onto the dance floor—and whatever you do, don't sit down on one of them or you'll be going aloft. Or you can close your eyes, hold on tight and try to get as caught up in the moment as the people who are carrying you around in the chair are. You may actually end up having fun.

Chapter 11
Invitations and Gifts

Q: The stationer that was printing our invitations has gone out of business.

A: Before you freak out, does your stationer have another location that you could visit instead? Is it possible that the stationer just closed the store you were using but kept other locations open in the meantime? If the business is gone for good, do you at least have records of what they ordered for you and when? If so, you may be able to contact the supplier directly—that is, the company that is printing your invitations, programs, and whatever else you'd ordered through your stationer—and see if they can't arrange for another store to work with you to fill your order. Or you may even be able to negotiate things so that the supplier ships your order to you directly. One of these options should put your original invitation order in your hands in time for the wedding.

Another option is to check with a national printing company such as Sir Speedy or Kinkos, and find out what kind of wedding-related services they might offer. With locations all over the place, national companies such as these are less likely to go under before your wedding occurs.

If none of these options work out, let me offer you this positive thought: We live in a great day and age of do-it-yourself everything—including wedding invitations. With a personal computer and a good printer, plus paper stock purchased from an office supply store such as **Staples** or a crafts chain such as Michaels or A.C. Moore, you should be able to whip up your own wedding invitations, programs, place cards, and thank-you notes without leaving the comfort of your home. So if your out-of-business stationer leaves you no options, at least you can take comfort in knowing that you (or someone computer savvy you know) can make your invitations at home.

Now about the money that you likely lost when the stationer went out of business: I really hope that you paid for your order by credit card. Why? You'll have the law on your side in recovering your money—especially if you paid for your entire invitation order up front and now have nothing to show for it. See page 61 for information about how the Fair Credit Billing Act can help.

In the meantime, a credit card-paying customer can dispute the charge with her credit card company—which means you won't have to pay for the invitations that weren't delivered and you won't accrue any interest on that charge while the credit card company investigates the situation. Either way—between the Fair Credit Billing Act and the muscle of MasterCard (or Visa, Discover, or American Express), you should be covered.

Q: We just discovered that the stationer didn't place our order. Now it's too late to get the invitations, thank-you notes, and programs we wanted.

A: Any chance that either of you is computer savvy? If so, you can make everything that you need for your wedding using your computer. Plenty of office supply stores, such as Staples, Office Depot, and OfficeMax, and craft supply stores such as Michaels and A.C. Moore, carry fine quality paper and cards that are designed to be used in an ink-jet or laser-jet printer for do-it-yourself wedding invitations, programs, place cards or anything else that you could possibly need printed for your wedding.

In a time bind and afraid of technology? Then tap into the expertise of nationwide companies such as Kinkos, or Internet printing shop *VistaPrint.com*, which can provide high-quality printed products for low prices—and in a quick turnaround time. (The one caveat with VistaPrint is that some of its lowest-price materials include a VistaPrint logo on them, so check with the company about this policy and whether or not it applies to invitation orders.)

❦

Q: I'm a habitual bargain shopper and even though we've ordered our invitations, I kept shopping around. Well, yesterday I found someplace that would handle them for a cheaper price. Am I stuck with my original decision?

A: You've really got to weigh the pros and cons of the situation before you make your decision. But before you do that, tell me: Has your original stationer already ordered your invitations and are they due to arrive any day now? If so, then changing stationers to save a couple of bucks will probably cost you more money in the end because you'll likely have to pay for the original order that you'll no longer want. However, if you've only left a deposit with the original stationer—and it would be cheaper for you in the long run to risk losing the deposit to use this other stationer—then making the change might make the most fiscal sense.

But you've got to be talking a really significant savings to justify the hassle and stress of going with a new stationer. Haven't you already spent a considerable amount of time choosing fonts, paper stocks, and invitation inserts? Are you willing to go through all of that again? Or can this other stationer order the exact same invitation set, programs, place cards, thank-you notes, and so on—and still save a significant amount of money?

For example, if the first stationer was going to charge you $10 per invitation set and the new stationer will only charge $5 per set, that's a significant savings. Are you confident you'll get the same (or better) quality printed materials than you would have from the first stationer? And does this other stationer have the reputation to support the price savings he is offering? Remember that sometimes things that seem too good to be true, such as really inexpensive (by comparison) invitations *are* too good to be true and will end up disappointing you in the end. Do you know others who've used this stationer and were happy with the products and service? Ask around and make sure you're making the best decision possible, not just the best money-saving decision. If saving some money up front means more hassles at the back end, I don't think making a change is worth it. Time is most definitely money when planning a wedding, and sometimes, if your budget can handle it, paying a little bit more for something such as invitations and other printed materials ends up making everything worth it in the end.

Q: It's eight weeks before the wedding, and we still haven't gotten our invitations from the stationer. Everything needs to go out today!

A: Why are you waiting for the last minute? Get on the phone now and find out what's going on. Luckily, you still have a small window of time to get your invitations out. Ideally, they should be out eight weeks before the wedding, but it won't kill you to send them out seven or six weeks before the wedding. However, the longer you wait to mail them, the less time you give your guests to send their RSVPs.

Now, if you call your stationer and discover that the invitations won't be in on time, you're going to have to make a quick decision. You can:

- A. Ask the stationer to expedite the order—and insist that they eat the extra costs since it was likely their mistake that delayed the order.
- B. Make your own invitations on your computer (visit an office supply or craft store for paper stock).
- C. Call a speedy printer and see if they can't turn around your order in the requisite time.
- D. Send out electronic invitations—especially if nearly all of your guests have access to e-mail. Sure, it may not be traditional or as pretty as a printed invitation, but it will get the job done—in that it will communicate the who, what, where, and when of your wedding in a timely manner.

Q: The stationer didn't print enough invitations.

A: Are you sure about that? I ask because when I ordered invitations for my wedding, I thought that the stationer had messed up and ordered too few invitations at first. Then it dawned on me—while I was inviting 200 people to my wedding, I only needed to mail out a little more than 100 invitations. This was because most of the people I was inviting were part of a couple or a family that lived at the same address—and each couple or family only needed to receive one invitation. Yes, I know that sounds like a ridiculous thing to do, but I know that I'm not the only bride who's ever made that mistake. So make sure that you didn't try to do some funky wedding math as I did.

If you didn't—and your stationer did end up shortchanging you on invitations (and you have written proof that she ordered too few)—you should insist that she order additional invitations to make up the difference (and that she do it fast), and she should eat the additional cost. There's no reason that you shouldn't be able to mail all of your invitations on time because she didn't place the order properly.

If for some reason she can't get you the extra invitations on time, then you've got to order some additional ones right away. Check with a national printing company such as Kinkos or Sir Speedy about getting the job done, or, if you're good with computers and design, consider creating and printing the additional invitations yourself on your computer. (You can find all the supplies you need at an office supply store such as Office Depot, Office Max, or Staples or a craft store such as Michaels or A.C. Moore—even mass-marketers such as Target and Wal-Mart carry these supplies.)

Q: I started assembling my invitations and discovered that the stationer didn't provide enough envelopes.

A: The first thing you should do is place a call to your stationer. Find out if she has any overstocks of your specific envelopes (or at least similar envelopes that will work in a pinch). If she doesn't—and she forgot to order the correct amount of envelopes—then request that she expedite an order of additional envelopes and suggest that she pick up the tab for the shipping. I'm sure mistakes with envelopes happen all the time, so asking her to get more in a pinch shouldn't be too much of a hassle.

In addition, I always advise brides to order 10 percent more envelopes than the invitations that they're ordering—and your stationer should have suggested you do so as well. Why? It's always possible for an envelope to get ruined or for the calligrapher to make a mistake while addressing an envelope. That's why you want to have extras on hand—when you make a mistake, you won't have to run around in a crazed state, trying to track down additional envelopes. You'll already have those extras there and can continue assembling or addressing your invitations as necessary.

Now let's say the stationer doesn't have any extra envelopes or isn't willing to get you them. You need these envelopes and you need them fast. Can you visit an office supply store or another stationery store to see if they have similar envelopes in stock? What about a paper supplier, such as the catalog PaperDirect or a Website such as *paperdirect.com* or *staples.com*? You may be able to find the exact envelopes you need and in no time.

As far as your stationer's behavior is concerned, you should address it (no pun intended) but do so after the wedding, when the stress of the big day is gone. If you haven't paid your invitation bill in full, I wouldn't rush to do so. How she treated you is unacceptable, and she should have made good on her mistake of ordering too few envelopes. If you have paid your bill in full—and paid it by credit card, I hope—I would dispute the charge with the credit card company. She didn't deliver the order as promised, and therefore she shouldn't receive full payment for half a job done.

Q: The stationer printed everything—invitations, place cards, and programs—on the wrong card stock. It's not what I wanted.

A: I'm sorry to hear that your stationer ended up using the wrong card stock, but can you live with the mistake? In other words, did you order an ecru stock but got white instead? I believe that as long as the paper stock is pretty close to what you asked for, you can make do with it—and you should. You shouldn't add more stress to an already stressful time by reordering your printed materials at the last minute. In the long run, no one is going to know that you got white instead of ecru, nor are they going to remember the color of the invitation they received. It may be hard for you to believe that, but it's true. Now if the stationer ordered bright pink paper instead of a cream, then you've got an issue, and the stationer should fix the problem pronto and for free.

Even if you decide to live with the stationer's mistake, you should request that he or she take some money off your order. There's no reason that you should have to pay full price for someone else's mistake. If the stationer refuses, you have two choices.

Your first option is to refuse to take possession of and pay for the order—and then dispute the charge with your credit card company. (You are paying for your invitations, programs, and place cards with a credit card, aren't you? You should so you have the muscle of the Fair Credit Billing Act behind you.) If you decide to forego the ordered invitations, I'm confident you can create professional-looking programs, invitations and place cards using paper stock purchased at an office supply store or craft store, and printing them on your home computer.

Your second option is to take the invitations and additional printed materials and use them for your wedding as planned. Then after the wedding, dispute the charge for the goods and services that your stationer didn't deliver as promised—and then report his unwillingness to work with you to both your state's Attorney General's office and the Better Business Bureau, both of which track unfair business practices. Even if you can't fix what happened with your invitation order, you can at least warn other customers to steer clear of this business in the future so they don't find themselves in a similar situation.

Q: The calligrapher didn't make enough place cards.

A: How much time do you have before the wedding? Any chance you have extra blank place cards? You can do one of two things—finish the job and just live with the fact that the handwriting won't match. Or you can toss all that she did and start from scratch.

While it's a lovely idea to have a calligrapher elegantly write each guest's name on his or her place card, when it comes down to it, it's not really necessary. A place card doesn't have the same weight or importance, if you will, as an invitation, which is likely going to sit out on someone's desk or on a bulletin board for weeks to come before your wedding. That's the sort of printed item you want to look very nice and to make a good impression, and that's why couples are usually so careful to pick the perfect invitation, card stock, and font. But a place card—well, it's there to tell someone where to sit at your reception, and once the person looks at it, picks it up, and finds his seat, its purpose is done. So if you end up handwriting each place card in your own scrawl, don't sweat it. No one is going to judge you or the quality of your wedding based on the place cards.

However, if you really hate your handwriting and don't relish the thought of handwriting each place card, look into place-card printing kits for the computer. You can find these at office supply stores, stationers, and craft supply stores. These come with a software template that will allow you to type each person's name in and then print them out in the font of your choice. For the computer-savvy bride, this may be your best timesaving option in the long run.

And make sure that after the wedding is over, you let the calligrapher know exactly how you feel about her messing up on the job. If you haven't paid her in full, don't. If you have—and can't get your money back—I would definitely report her bad behavior to the Better Business Bureau and the state's Attorney General's office. You want to warn brides- and grooms-to-be that this is a calligrapher not to be trusted.

Q: I don't understand what happened—the calligrapher addressed the invitations wrong and they need to go out today.

A: It's possible that your calligrapher overbooked herself, was juggling too many wedding jobs at once, and addressed your invitations for someone else's wedding. Can you call her and find out if this is what happened? Can you also ask if your set of invitation envelopes might be with another couple—and, by chance, they're the same size and card stock as your invitations? If so—and I realize that's a stretch—perhaps she can arrange a switch. She should also offer to discount her fee because of her very large mistake, and I hope that she does.

Now let's say that you can't make the switch. Probably your best bet is to do this: Go to an office supply store and purchase mailing labels. Then create a mailing list for all of your guests, print it in a wedding-like font on those mailing labels, and get the invitations in the mail. If your envelopes are at all salvageable, choose larger-size mailing labels so you can stick them right over the wrong addresses. If the envelopes are not salvageable, you're going to have to invest in a whole new set of invitation envelopes (which you can likely find in a similar color and paper stock at an office supply store or a stationer's shop) and stick the mailing labels on those.

Those solutions take care of the mailing envelopes. For the inner envelopes, you can try the mailing-label route or you can simply hand write everyone's name on a new set of inner envelopes.

I'm sorry that you had this problem, and I hope your calligrapher can do whatever's possible to help fix the problem—from tracking down additional envelopes to discounting her fee to make up for the gaffe. Also, in the future, whenever you need to hire a calligrapher, make sure that you budget enough time to proof the job. The last thing you should do is to plan to have the calligrapher deliver the invitations on the very day they need to get them into the mail. By giving yourself a week or so leeway, you'll have enough time to fix any problems should they arise, as happened with these incorrectly addressed invitations.

> ### Wedding Wisdom
>
> One of my husband's work colleagues RSVPd for our wedding to my husband at work but never sent back his RSVP card. Then my husband forgot to tell me that his coworker and his wife would be joining us at the wedding. So we arrived at the reception to find them standing around. Of course, there was no place card for them or a place for them to eat dinner. Luckily, two people that were supposed to join us canceled at the last minute, so we seated them at that table.
> —Laura, New York

Q: Our invitations and programs arrived saying Jane Smith and Michael Jones, but I'm Jan and he's Mark. How could they get this wrong?

A: Did your stationer fax you a proof of your invitation for approval before he sent them to the printer? If not, he should have. I've known way too many brides who discovered an *a.m.* instead of a *p.m.* on their wedding invitations or a misspelled name in a proof, which they had the chance to fix before all the invitations were printed. Had your stationer sent you a rough copy to proof, you would have noticed that he got your names wrong.

So you're stuck with invitations with your names wrong on them. Can your stationer expedite a new set of invitations with the correct information on them? And is he willing to do this and eat the cost for this costly mistake? I surely hope so.

If not, you can either make an entirely new set of invitations yourself or place an order with a quick printing shop or online company that's sure to get you your invitations on time.

If the do-it-yourself route seems like a good idea, you can visit an office supply store, such as Staples, Office Depot, or OfficeMax, or a mass-merchandiser, such as Target or Wal-Mart, for your supplies. These stores carry fine quality papers designed for creating wedding invitations on an ink-jet or laser-jet printer. (At these stores, you can also find paper stock and printing templates for programs, place cards, or anything else that you could possibly need printed for your wedding.)

If you'd rather have someone else be responsible for the printing job, then turn to a company such as Kinkos or the Internet printing shop *VistaPrint.com*, which can provide high-quality printed products for low prices—and in a quick turn-around.

One recent bride I know used the company Wedding.Orders (*www.wedding.orders.com*), which specializes in major brands, themes, color schemes, and has an overnight delivery option. She was able to design the invitation, write it, proofread it, choose the number she needed, etc. She had everything sent overnight to ensure that if there were any problems, she would have the time to correct them.

Q: Nobody is "RSVPing" to the wedding. What? No one likes us?

A: Unfortunately, in today's modern world, bad manners abound. People rarely RSVP on time, if they RSVP at all, and no one seems to appreciate the very serious nature of an RSVP request and deadline. A bride asks her guests to RSVP so she'll know how many people are coming to the event, and so she can order everything needed for the wedding—from programs to place cards to pass-around hors d'oeuvres. I'm sorry to hear that your guests aren't sending back their RSVP cards on time, but, then again, I'm not surprised.

Okay, so your RSVP date has come and gone, and you've barely got a skeleton of a guest list. It's time to start following up with people. I hope that when you made your invitation list, you also jotted down people's phone numbers and e-mail addresses. If not, you're going to have to collect them now, because you need them.

Begin by calling each unresponsive person. Don't yell at people for not responding. Instead, let them know that you understand how busy everyone is these days and that you're sorry to bother them, but you really need to know now whether or not they'll be coming to your wedding. I'm sure most people will apologize left and right about forgetting to respond, and most will be able to give you their answer straight away.

For those who don't know or whom you can't reach on the phone (and have to leave a voice mail), let them know that you'll check back with them in a few days. Then do it. Or send them a follow-up e-mail, with your phone number, so they'll have two ways of getting in touch with you. Be persistent with your tardy guests, and soon enough you'll know exactly who is coming to your wedding and who isn't.

Q: People are buying our registry gifts from stores other than where we registered. How can I stop them?

A: First, you should be thankful that your guests are being so generous and buying so many of the gifts off of your registry list. Sure, it's a bummer that they're buying them from stores other than where you registered, but let me ask you: Did you register for a range of items that cost a little to a lot? I always suggest that couples register for a wide selection of gifts. Why? Not every guest who is invited to your wedding can afford to spend a lot of money on your engagement, bridal shower, or wedding gift. Your parents and family members may want to splurge on your new china or a set of silver, but if you have friends in graduate school or a cousin who is just starting out at her first job, they'll appreciate finding affordable items on your registry list.

Here's another question you should answer: Did you register at stores that are convenient for your guests? This is equally as important as registering for a wide range of items so that guests won't have a hard time accessing your registry list and shopping for your gifts.

So if you registered at a store with only one location—and a large portion of your guests happen to live far away from this store—they probably had no option but to shop elsewhere. Here's what your guests probably did. They started their shopping for your wedding gifts by calling the store where you registered and asked to have your registry list faxed, e-mailed, or mailed to them. Then they took that list to other stores near them or comparison-shopped on the Web, and then made their purchases accordingly.

To avoid receiving duplicate gifts from your registry, always register for inexpensive as well as expensive items (and everything in between). Also, register your preferences with at least two stores. Make sure that one of the stores is a national retailer or has a strong online presence or Website on which guests can easily access your registry list and shop. Remember: You want to make your guests gift-buying experience as easy and as affordable as possible. If you do your homework up front and select stores that know how to work with all kinds of wedding guests, you're sure to have a great gift-registry experience.

Q: The store at which we registered isn't letting us return extras from our registry list. That doesn't seem like very good customer service!

A: It sounds like perfectly *awful* customer service. One of the reasons that couples register for gifts is to make gift-buying easier for their wedding guests. One of the reasons that stores set up gift-registry programs is so they can establish long-term relationships with the bride, groom, and all of their guests—ideally, by making their shopping experience as pleasant as possible. If the store is making things difficult instead of easy, you need to find a manager and get your problem fixed—pronto. If you don't find satisfaction at the store level, find out who a regional-level store manager is, and keep pressing people at the store until they take back the gifts.

Now this is all assuming that the gifts you've tried to return come from that store. If they come from another retailer, then you really don't have any right to expect the store to take the items back. Today, more and more stores are cracking down on unauthorized returns and refusing to give credit if you try to return something without a receipt. So keep that in mind if you ever are invited to a wedding and are tempted to buy a registry item at a store other than where the couple registered. At least do the decent thing and enclose a gift receipt so that should they need to make a return, they'll know where you got the gift and they'll be able to get full credit for your purchase.

Q: Where I grew up, people sent wedding gifts to the bride's or the groom's parents' home. Now everyone is showing up with gifts in hand. How are we going to get all these packages home?

A: It's interesting when you learn that wedding gift-giving practices vary by region. For example, I grew up in the Northeast where everyone gives money to the happy couple. Then I moved to the Midwest for a couple of years and discovered that the favored wedding gift was an item off the registry, not a gift of money.

Recently I attended a wedding in New York City where many of the guests came from the Midwest. They kept asking where the gift table was, because they had wrapped gifts they wanted to put down somewhere. Unfortunately, the bride, who'd never lived outside of New York City and had always given money as a gift, hadn't planned for this gift contingency. Before she knew it, wrapped boxes started piling up around the dais table, because there was nowhere else to put them.

Every bride, regardless of where she grew up or where she's getting married, should plan for both gift situations—people handing her and her new husband envelopes (with the gift of money inside) and people coming to the wedding bearing boxed gifts. She should have a safe place to keep the money gifts and a table or room where people can put boxed gifts. Similarly, she should plan to have someone be the designated gift guard (anyone from an attendant, a trusted friend, or the catering manager), if you will, or the person who will be responsible for taking the gifts home from the reception. That way the couple won't end up like you did—overloaded with wedding gifts and no way to get them home.

Q: I can't believe it—I lost the money bag. Now what do I do?

A: Assuming you lost the money purse during your reception, this is where your deejay or bandleader can come in handy. Ask him to make an announcement to your guests, so that everyone can be on alert for the money purse. It's likely that one of the servers or guests moved it without realizing it. Recently, I was at a wedding where the mother of the bride put her purse down on a chair while having her picture taken—then came back a few minutes later to find it was gone. Turns out no one stole it; She'd just put it down on a chair that the caterer moved to one of the dinner tables she was setting up, and once they'd retraced that chair's steps (thanks to the catering manager's help), they found the mother's purse.

To avoid losing a money purse in the future, make sure you either have a designated keeper of the purse or the purse itself has a handle on it that you can wrap around your wrist for safekeeping. The idea is to make sure someone always knows where it is, and then you won't have to worry about losing it.

Another very popular option that brides are utilizing is the oversized antique birdhouse. They can be rented at craft stores (or even bridal centers or at the shops that sell dyeable shoes) or created using a white birdcage (a craft store find). The florist can include some flowers to decorate its table or area. This is a great option because, not only is the money in a very sizable container (hard to lose), but the envelopes are slipped through the tiny openings between the bars, preventing the loss of a card and making the bride and groom's task of collecting the cards nonexistent.

Q: I can't find the gifts I was going to give to the wedding party, my parents, or my new husband.

A: I can only imagine how crazed the morning of your wedding was. You probably thought that you'd have plenty of time to give out these gifts to the important people in your life, but then the hairdresser and makeup artist arrived, your wedding party showed up, and, before you knew it, it was time to get dressed and leave for the wedding. So is it possible that you simply misplaced those gifts or left them behind in the hotel room or the house where you got ready that morning? See if you can't get someone to retrace your steps and track down those missing gifts.

If they are truly gone, you've just got to laugh the whole thing off—and then explain to all the planned gift recipients exactly what happened. Everyone who's ever been in or had a wedding knows how crazy things can get. By being upfront about the misplaced gifts, I'm sure everyone will appreciate your honesty and not come away offended because you don't have a gift for them.

Another way to avoid this is to give gifts out at the rehearsal dinner. The day will most likely move at a slower pace than it will on the day of the wedding, and, if the bridal attendants gifts are jewelry, cufflinks, ties, or shawls to wear at the wedding, they will have time to put them to good use.

Q: I can't believe I've lost the favors we were going to give to our guests. Help!

A: If there's one thing that should be a snap to replace at the last minute, it's the favors. Sure, you may have thought long and hard about the token of appreciation you're going to give to your guests for coming to your wedding—and now you're running to the store to find something, anything, so your guests don't leave empty-handed.

Here are some quick and easy last-minute favor ideas:

- A simple votive and clear, glass holder, available at a craft store.
- Scattering Hershey Kisses or another kind of candy on the reception tables—giving you not only favors, but sweet decorations as well.
- Putting packets of wildflower seeds in small terra-cotta pots. (You can even tie a ribbon around the pot that matches your bridesmaids' dresses.)

If you simply don't have the time to run to a store and buy favors in bulk, you can always make a donation to a favorite charity in your guests' honor. Check out the Websites of the I Do Foundation (*idofoundation.org*) and Married For Good (*marriedforgood.com*) for good causes that will gladly become the benefactor of your wedding generosity. If you go this route, then the only thing you'll need to do is print up cards to place on the reception tables, letting folks know that instead of traditional favors, you've made a charitable donation.

Q: We were in such a hurry to open gifts that we didn't keep a list of who gave us what. Now we don't know how to handle our thank-you notes.

A: I understand how easy it is to get caught up in the moment of opening gifts. After my wedding reception, my husband and I had less than an hour to open our gifts before we had to leave for the airport for our honeymoon. We were so excited about opening our gifts that we started tearing into a few of them before we caught ourselves. Rather than let things get too crazy, I grabbed a pad of paper and a pen (you could use the inside of one of your cards), and designated myself as the gift-list writer. Bill, who felt like the proverbial kid on Christmas morning, designated himself the gift opener, and together we got through all the gifts in no time and created a comprehensive gift list that made writing our thank-you notes a snap. I recommend that every couple use this dual approach when opening gifts. That way you won't end up stressing out how to handle your notes of thanks because you're not sure of each gift's origin.

The best way you can handle your thank-you notes is to write them promptly and with a gracious message (albeit a generic one, because you're not sure of who gave you what). Try something such as this:

Dear Sue and Bill:
Thank you so much for joining us at our wedding and
for your lovely gift. We appreciate your celebrating with
us and hope to see you both soon.
Thanks again.

This is a simple note of thanks that conveys your gratitude without giving away the fact that you have no idea what Sue and Bill actually gave you.

Q: I forgot that the postage went up. Now all the invitations are coming back "return to sender" and I know that I don't have enough postage on my RSVP cards. Yikes!

A: I'm surprised that when you went to your local postal service branch to buy the "love" stamps that I'm sure you used to mail your wedding invitations, the postal clerk didn't warn you of the impending postal rate hike. He should of, and I'm sorry that his mistake is causing you such grief. Because it could take the postal service a week or so to return the invitations for additional postage—which they're likely to do—I would be proactive about the situation and call all of your guests. Let them know that there was a small mistake with sufficient postage on your invitations, and they're going to be delayed. Use the phone call as a "save the date" call, if you will, so that you can at least notify your guests of the time, date, and location of your wedding, and ask them to be on the lookout for your invitations. You could get lucky and have the postal service decide to deliver your invitations with a "postage due" notice for the recipients. Not a great impression to make on your invited guests, but you can make up for it in your thank-you notes—you can include a stamp equaling the amount of the postage difference as a sort of "mea culpa" to your guests to forgive you for your postage snafu on your invitations.

Now as far as your RSVP cards go, you might be able to sneak that one out—if the "to" and "from" addresses on the envelopes are the same. That is, if the postal service tries to return the cards to sender because of insufficient postage—and the sender's address is the same as the recipient's (your address)—then all the cards will get to you just fine.

Finally, to avoid problems such as this in the future, always take an invitation set to the post office before you send out the whole lot. This trip to the post office will accomplish two things: One, it will allow the postal clerk to weigh your invitation set so you'll know exactly how much postage you need. And, two, it will give you a chance to double- check that there won't be any postage hikes in the near future that could adversely affect your invitation mailing.

Wedding Wisdom

I never double-checked the cross street of the chapel where we were having our ceremony and just put what I thought was the correct street on the invitation. Well, I was wrong. I didn't discover my mistake until I was on the way to the chapel on my wedding day. Luckily, everyone figured it out and arrived in time.
—Jillian, Pennsylvania

Chapter 12
Flowers, Rings, and Transportation

Flowers

Q: The florist with whom I ordered our flowers has put down roots in another town and says I'm too far away for him to do my wedding now.

A: Can this florist recommend any other florists near you that can offer similar blooms and bouquets and work with a similar budget? Make sure that you ask. In many businesses, such as floral arranging, everyone knows everyone. Even though your florist may have seen other businesses as his competition, he may also have developed a good working relationship with one or two other professionals in his field and may be able to send you to someone who will treat you as well (if not better) than he could.

Also, what kind of agreement did you have with this florist? If you've taken my advice so far and gotten everything in writing from your vendors, your agreement with your florist should cover you. Reread it to find out if he might still be responsible for supplying the flowers for your wedding (from afar, no less than) or at least for returning the deposit. Or if you paid for the flowers in full and in advance by credit card, you should dispute the charge so you don't have to pay for goods and services the florist will not be supplying.

If your original florist is no help at all, then you're going to have to start back at square one like you did when you were first researching florists. Ask every recently married couple you know in your area which florist they used and if they were happy with how everything went. Perhaps your reception site can help you find another florist as well. Have you recently received or ordered flowers for someone—and were extremely impressed with the florist's business savoir-faire or presentation skills? If so, see if this company does weddings and find out if they're available and willing to work with you. There are plenty of bridal shows (Bridal Expo in a nationally held show) where you can view samples, talk with vendors, and speak with other brides and their families about florists (as well as other vendors). Also, Websites such as *weddingchannel.com* offer links and recommendations for all vendors and aspects of the event. Remember: What one person might call the most beautiful arrangement, you may think is the worst on the planet!

Take Website recommendations with a grain of salt. These kinds of sites can be a good starting point if you find yourself in a bind, but they should not be your "be all, end all" for finding a florist. As long as you keep asking questions and checking references of the florist (or any other vendor you may hire for your wedding), you're sure to find a florist who will make your wedding look fabulous.

Q: We called our florist to ask them a question and discovered that they didn't actually book us for the date we'd agreed on. He thinks he can squeeze us in, but won't be able to get all of the flowers I want.

A: If you love your florist, feel as though he's giving you the best price possible, and you can live without some of the flowers you wanted, then why make your life more complicated by firing your florist? Yes, he screwed up by forgetting to book your date, but at least he's trying to make good on the deal by working with you anyway. Make sure you find out from him exactly what kinds of blooms he can get for you—and that his substitutions are okay with you. Also, given that this snafu is his fault, he should offer you some kind of discount on his service or throw in something extra to make up for the fact that you're going to have to compromise on flower choices because of his mistake.

However, if the florist is neither gracious nor forgiving about the whole situation—and is making you feel like you should be lucky to have him decorating your wedding—then I say get rid of him. He sounds like a prima donna anyway.

Also, if he forgot to book your wedding—and only remembered because you called to ask him a question—think about what will happen on your wedding day? Will you have to call him on your cell phone, on the way to the ceremony, to make sure that he's showing up? You don't want to have any doubts about any of the vendors you've hired for your wedding. So if you're at all unsure about this florist—or aren't happy with the makeshift goods he's offering—then find someone else to provide the flowers for your wedding. You'll probably find yourself happier in the end.

Q: I'm a habitual bargain shopper and even though we booked our florist, I kept shopping around. Well, yesterday I found a cheaper florist. Now what?

A: Just because the florist is cheaper doesn't mean she'll do a better job with the flowers for your wedding. Are you certain she can provide the same exact blooms that your original florist can? Do you know for sure that the flowers she'll deliver will arrive on time looking fresh? How much do you really know about this florist, beyond the fact that her prices are better than your original florist? Don't let dollar signs affect your decision-making savvy when it comes to your wedding.

The old adage "You get what you pay for" really does come true quite often and is something to seriously consider when booking any vendor for your wedding. So if your original florist is a bit more expensive, but you know and trust her—and know she'll come through for you on your big day—then stay with the florist you know. You'll be able to sleep easier knowing your flower order will arrive just as you'd planned. However, if this other florist has a track record that you find impressive—many brides have recommended her to you and raved about her great prices, phenomenal flowers, and super service—then it might be worth considering a switch.

But before you tear up your contract with your original florist and book this new florist, make sure the original florist hasn't already put in a special order for your flowers—which you'll probably have to pick up the tab for, even though you're canceling. Also, did you put down a nonrefundable deposit that you'll lose when you cancel? And will the deposit that you're about to lose make up the difference in the savings you would have received from the new florist? If so, then stick with your original florist, because you won't gain anything by making the switch.

> ### *Wedding Wisdom*
>
> During my reception, I noticed that I didn't have a "throwaway" bouquet for the bouquet toss. I calmly told the DJ about my situation so he wouldn't announce the bouquet toss—just yet. Then I turned to my bridesmaids to help come up with a solution. We found some leftover flowers that had decorated the cocktail area, and we quickly fashioned them in a makeshift, throwaway bouquet. My bouquet toss went perfectly.
> —Annette, Ohio

Q: What if the florist orders the wrong flowers for everything?

A: The best way to avoid any surprises on your wedding day is to keep in constant communication with your vendors and to make sure that they put everything in writing for you to review before placing any orders. I'm sure your caterer faxed you a menu for approval ahead of time, and your stationer faxed you a proof of your invitation wording for your okay.

Your florist should do the same, especially if you're special ordering off-season flowers (which will likely cost more and have to be shipped from some faraway location) or requesting very specific blooms for your bouquet, boutonnieres, corsages, centerpieces, and more. Why not request that the florist create a sample arrangement? You'll be able to ensure you understand what he is explaining to you, guarantee that you adore what you are ordering, and prevent any miscommunications.

If your florist balks at the idea of faxing you the flower order ahead of time for your approval, or creating a sample arrangement, then I would suggest finding another florist. All you're doing is asking to double check the order so you can feel confident that you're getting the flowers you want. If the florist tries to brush you off by telling you, "Don't worry. I've got everything under control," I would be very worried and I might second-guess that florist as my best choice for my wedding.

Now let's say you do all that—double-check the order, communicate frequently with your florist, etc.—and you get to your wedding and the flowers are all wrong. Close your eyes. Take a deep breath in. Then exhale. Now open your eyes and remember: You know exactly what your flowers are supposed to look like, and possibly so does your maid of honor or mother. But you're probably the only ones. The rest of your wedding guests won't know that you ordered calla lilies but got lily of the valley instead. Yes, the florist messed up but on the day of the wedding, it's too late to fix the problem, so please don't freak out.

As long as the flowers got there on time, arrived in sufficient quantities, and looked pretty, then you should just go ahead with your wedding day and don't let the flower faux pas ruin your day. Later, after you return from the honeymoon, you can take the issue up with the florist and see if she will make up for her mess up, such as by refunding some of your money or giving you free flower deliveries on your next order for a birthday or other special occasion.

Q: How are people with allergies supposed to have bridal bouquets?

A: No one ever said that a bridal or bridesmaid bouquet has to be made from fresh flowers. If you or any of your attendants are allergic to flowers, I would recommend you avoid fresh flowers all together. Instead, find a florist who specializes in silk flowers. I've seen a number of beautiful bouquets with silk flowers in them, which I had a hard time believing they were not real because they were so lifelike. Have the florist use silk flowers for all of your decorations, including in the church, the boutonnieres, and the table centerpieces. That way, the allergic bride or groom won't be sneezing "ah-choo" when they should be saying "I do" instead. Also, by using silk flowers, your bouquet will last forever and make a terrific keepsake from your wedding day.

Q: We have fresh flowers on all the tables of our outdoor reception, and now there are bees swarming everywhere.

A: I recently read a survey that said September had surpassed June as the most popular wedding month. What that means for brides planning a September wedding is they'll also be planning a wedding during yellow-jacket season—and they should take the necessary precautions to avoid swarms of bees at the wedding or reception.

One such precaution would be to avoid an outdoor wedding reception. Like ants to a picnic basket, yellow jackets come out of the woodwork whenever you eat outside. If you want to save your guests the hassle, serve your food indoors—or at least late in the evening when yellow jackets are less likely to be actively flying around.

If you must have your reception outside, try to work some sort of bee repellant into your centerpiece, such as a candle designed to keep bees away. You may also want to avoid brightly colored flowers that will attract more buzzing buddies to your reception and go with something that bees won't find as attractive. (Speak to your florist or catering manager about centerpiece options in this regard. They should have plenty of experience recommending table decorations that help keep the bees at bay.)

Finally, if you know that any of your guests are allergic to bees, insert a special note in their invitation or call them directly to let them know that you're going to be having an outdoor wedding reception. This will give them ample notice to bring along any medication they may need to take in case of a bee sting. In addition, it's probably a good idea to have a first-aid kit on hand so that if a bee stings anyone, you can deal with it appropriately. (Speak to your pharmacist about what she would suggest you stock in the first-aid kit for treating bee stings and other minor injuries someone might sustain at a wedding.)

> ### Wedding Wisdom
>
> We got to the wedding ceremony location and found that the florist had not delivered the correct number of corsages for the grandmothers. We sent the boyfriend of one of my bridesmaids across the street to a florist shop and had him buy emergency ones. I don't think anyone noticed they weren't the same.
> —Brette, New York

Rings

Q: The jewelry store where we'd ordered our rings from went out of business. Now, we have no rings for the wedding and, worst of all, our down payment is gone along with our rings.

A: Did you at least pay for your rings with a credit card? If so, you may be able to dispute the charge with the credit card company or use the Fair Credit Billing Act of 1974 (which protects consumers against unauthorized credit card charges or, in the case of your missing jeweler and missing wedding bands, "charges for goods and services [that] weren't delivered as agreed," according to the Federal Trade Commission (FTC) Website at *www.ftc.gov*. (The FTC enforces the Fair Credit Billing Act, so check out the Website for more information on how this act may cover you in this situation.)

Now onto the problem of your missing rings. Your best bet is to get on the telephone to local jewelers or to start asking your friends, family members, and coworkers if they can recommend a nearby jeweler who would be able to get you wedding bands in time for your nuptials. You may not be able to order the exact same rings that you'd chosen before, but at this point the most important thing is to have a set of rings that you can use on your wedding day. Besides, if you don't like the last-minute rings, you can always arrange to return them after the fact (if the jeweler will agree to this) and then order the bands you want when you're under less time pressure.

Jewelry exchanges are a good option because (buildings in which many vendors show their products) offer on-site sizing, cleaning, and buying of merchandise. You can purchase the exact ring you try on and usually for a cheaper price than major jewelers. Because each vendor is in direct competition with the counter next to them, explaining your story can drive prices way down (as can walking away a few times).

There are also Websites that offer quality rings (and overnight shipping). All the bride and groom would have to do is go to a jeweler to be sized so that they choose the correct size online. Blue Nile (*bluenile.com*) offers wedding bands as well as engagement rings (not that you need that right now). If time permits, Blue Nile can send a ring sizer so that you can feel 100-percent confident in ordering your ring size from them and their overnight shipping is free! In addition, the site offers suggestions for attendants' gifts—not too shabby if you've left that for the last minute, too.

Q: We called the jeweler to ask them a question about our rings and discovered that they hadn't placed the order on time. Now our rings won't be ready for the wedding. What can we do?

A: You have two choices: You can keep the order for the original rings and use decoys at your wedding. (Make sure the jeweler gives you a discount or makes up for their mistake in one way or another.) Or you can cancel your order with the original jeweler (check first that you can get a full refund of any money you'd paid for the missing rings) and buy rings "off the rack," if you will.

I realize that buying a wedding band in one day may be a bit harder than buying a wedding dress off the rack—not all jewelers keep inventory on the premises—but if you're stuck between having no rings on your wedding day or having something that is less than perfect, you'll have to decide which option seems the best for you and your fiancé.

Q: I'm a habitual bargain shopper and even though we've ordered our rings, I kept shopping around. Well, yesterday I found the same wedding bands for less. Am I stuck or what?

A: If your jeweler is like most jewelers, he's special-ordered your wedding bands—and probably put that order in the day you gave him a deposit for your rings. So call him and find out what would happen if you canceled your order. Would you lose your deposit by canceling? Would you get your money refunded because you notified him within a certain period of time? Will the jeweler be able to sell your rings to someone else or be willing to work out a consignment situation so that neither one of you loses money in the end? As long as you can answer each of these questions satisfactorily—and you're talking a significant savings on your rings to justify the hassle of switching jewelers—then it might make sense to make the switch.

However, if you saw your rings for what seemed like a "too good to be true" price, it might be—especially if you saw an advertisement in a magazine, newspaper, or on the Internet—and not in person. Be sure to thoroughly investigate this other jeweler and make sure it's a business on the up-and-up before you cancel your order with the original jeweler. The last thing I'd want to see happening to you is having you be without rings on your big day because you make a rash shopping decision, simply to save money.

Transportation

Q: The limousine company that was to take us to and from the wedding went out of business. Now, we have no way to get to the ceremony and reception, and, worst of all, our deposit is gone, too.

A: It's not right that this company left you stranded, and I'm sorry to hear about your transportation trouble. However, like most things for your wedding, I hope that you paid for your limousine deposit using a credit card. If so, call your credit card company and see if they can waive the charge (since the limousine company has disappeared) or at least help you track down the owners to get your money back.

Now to find another limousine. If you're having your wedding during a popular time, such as spring prom season, or the popular wedding months of June and September, you may have a difficult time booking a limousine at the last minute. Might you consider one of these alternate options? You could rent:

- A white Lincoln Town Car (or similar fancy automobile) that you can use to drive yourself to the wedding—or have a family member act as your chauffeur.
- A white classic car such as a Rolls Royce or a "fun" car, such as a PT Cruiser or VW Beetle, so you'll arrive at your wedding in unique style.
- A trolley to bring you and your entire wedding party to the church and reception.
- A horse and buggy, if weather permits and you don't have far to travel to your ceremony or reception.

There's no reason that you have to stay with the tried-and-true white limousine if you don't want to or circumstances won't let you. Consider some of these off-the-beaten-path options, and I'm confident you'll come up with a fun and functional solution to your transportation troubles.

Q: We called our limousine company to ask them a question and discovered that they didn't actually book us for the date we'd agreed on. Now our date is not available. What can we do?

A: I'd say be glad that you discovered that your limousine company is a disorganized operation well before your wedding—and not on the day of the wedding. My guess is that a company that forgets to book a wedding is a company that forgets to pick up the bride, the groom, or the wedding party. So find another limousine company to take you to your wedding, and make sure you go with a company that has a clean driving record, has few complaints lodged against them with the Better Business Bureau or your state's Attorney General's office, and comes highly recommended from people you know, like, and respect.

> ### Wedding Wisdom
>
> Our limousine driver "forgot" to pick up my brother and sister-in-law the morning of the wedding. My family kept this from us until late that evening, and my brother and sister-in-law handled it much better than I would have! Later we complained to the limo company, who almost two years later drove us to the Bruce Springsteen concert and back, free-of-charge!
> —Diane, Virginia

Q: I just discovered a cheaper limousine company. Will I lose my deposit if I go with the new company?

A: If you booked during a busy time for limousines—such as one of the popular wedding months of June or September or during prom season—the limousine company will likely make up the business if you cancel. However, precisely because it is their busy time and they may have turned away other clients because they had your wedding penciled in on their commitment list, they may charge you a penalty fee for canceling. These are all of the things you should keep in mind when considering changing limousine services for your wedding.

Although this new limousine company promises to save you money on its services, are you confident that they'll do as promised? Do you know other couples that have used this company—and can speak up for its reputation? Have you ever taken this car service before? If it's the company your employer uses to transport people and that's how you're getting a discount, you can probably feel pretty comfortable knowing that they'll do a good job of driving your wedding party around. Any smart company won't risk losing a corporate account by messing up someone's wedding. Just make sure that the money you'll save by using a different limousine company is worth it in the end. If you have to forego the vintage car you had your heart set on or if they don't have the stretch limousine you wanted, then you have to ask yourself: *Do I really want to save a couple of bucks or do I really want to arrive at my wedding in a certain style?* Only you will know the answer to those questions, and you should make a decision based on your gut—not just on your pocketbook.

Q: The limousine that was supposed to take us to the ceremony never showed up. We had to hail a taxi to the wedding. I never envisioned myself arriving at my wedding in a yellow cab.

A: You're not the only bride who was left stranded by her limousine company. I've heard of limousines that never arrived to take the wedding party to the reception, the bride and groom home from the reception, and limousines that left early because the ceremony or reception was running late and they needed to get to another gig.

When hiring a car service or limousine to transport people to and from your wedding, you should always ask about the following:

- Do you have a 24-hour customer service line that I can call in case of a problem?
- Do you own a fleet of multiple cars in case a car breaks down?
- Do you employ multiple drivers so that, should my driver become unavailable, you can send a replacement instead?
- How many events do you book per day/per driver?
- Are you able to offer an overflow window of opportunity should the ceremony or reception run late?

In addition to asking these very important questions, find out what the company's fee policy is should you need the limousine for longer than anticipated. Also, you should inquire about what kind of refund they might offer you if the car you originally requested isn't available and they have to send a replacement car that is of a lesser quality than the car you originally asked for. Finally, make sure you get all of this in writing, and have someone in your wedding party keep that contract, along with the limousine company's 24-hour hot line, with him or her at the wedding so if there is a problem, you'll know whom to call and what your rights are.

Q: Our limousine company gave us the option of choosing a non-smoking car, and we did. But when the driver showed up, he had a butt hanging from his lips and there were ashes strewn everywhere. Also, it looked like our limousine had come directly from another event. It was littered with beer bottles and just disgusting inside. Aren't companies supposed to clean the cars out first?

A: What does your contract with the car company say? Does it specify that it will clean each car in between events? While this sounds like a no-brainer—and good customer service for the limousine company—you can't assume that all those who own limousine companies or drive limos care about keeping the cars clean.

When researching the company that will take you to and from your wedding, you should always inquire about the state of their cars—and if they promise to provide a spiffy car upon arrival. There's a car service that I use for special events and business travel that I always book because I know that the drivers will arrive on time, they'll be dressed immaculately, and the cars will always be in tip-top shape—inside and out. That's the kind of car-service company you want to use for your wedding because no bride or groom should have to ride to a wedding, worrying that cigarette ashes or spilled beer will ruin their clothes.

In addition, you should inquire about how much time the car-service company allocates in between events. That way you'll know if there is sufficient time for the driver to vacuum out the interior or take the car for a quick washing.

Finally, should the limousine arrive in less-than-perfect condition and not at all as you'd specified in your contract, I would withhold a tip from the driver and, if you haven't paid for the limousine in full, withhold payment as well. Any business owner understands that people will talk about a negative experience with a company many more times over than a positive one. If the owner of this limousine company is smart, he'll try to make this mistake up to you in one way or another rather than risk bad word-of-mouth among your engaged friends who could conceivably be his customers in the near future. If he doesn't, don't be shy about reporting his less-than-stellar business practices to the local Better Business Bureau and your state's Attorney General's office—both of which track unfair business transactions.

Q: We ordered a specific special car to use on our wedding day and all the car company had on the actual day was a boring, old white car. I want my money back.

A: When you contracted this limousine company, did you put your specific car request in writing? If so, contractually the company should have fulfilled their obligation by providing the special car you requested—such as the vintage white Rolls Royce that you wanted and mentioned in the contract. I believe that the company should have come through on your original request—or at least given you notice that your desired car wasn't available. If they didn't you should ask for a discount on your rental fee. If that doesn't fly, then you should strongly suggest (in writing, naturally) that the company make up for their mistake by providing you with car service in the future for free.

Now let's say that your contract only specified a white car—and that's exactly what showed up on your big day. Then in reality the company held up their end of the bargain. Unfortunately, that doesn't leave you with very solid grounds for filing a complaint.

Q: The best man, who drove my husband to the wedding, left the reception with our car keys still in his pocket and now we have no way of getting home.

A: Are there any additional guests left at the wedding that can give you a lift? If not, can your reception hall call a cab for you? Might you be staying at a hotel that has shuttle service you can use? No one ever expects to get stranded at their own wedding, but it's a story I've heard often from brides—especially those who had weddings that ran late into the night. It's a good idea for the bride and groom to plan beforehand for how they're going to get home from their wedding. Think of it as your designated driver, but for a completely different reason. It could be that you simply ask your limousine to come back at a certain hour or you can plan to have a car service waiting to take you home. Better yet—book a honeymoon suite within walking distance of your reception site and then you won't have to rely on anyone or anything but your own two feet to get you home after your wedding reception.

Wedding Wisdom

My limos never showed up to take anyone to the church. We had booked three limos for the day: one to pick up the guys at the hotel and take them to the church at 3:00 for our 3:30 wedding, and two to come to my parents' house to pick up the girls. My dad had called the week before to confirm and everything was set...or so we thought. Since it was 3:15 and the limos weren't there, my mother called the limo company and explained the situation. The next thing I heard her say was, "What do you mean no limos are coming?" One of my bridesmaids stepped up and rallied all the girls to my mother's car, and drove them to the church. Everyone else drove themselves. What did I do? I rode shotgun in my photographer's SUV to the church. At least it was a white SUV.
—Jen, New Jersey

Chapter 13
The Honeymoon

Q: The travel agency we'd used to book our honeymoon went out of business. Now we have no plans for our honeymoon and, worst of all, we'd paid for the trip in full.

A: The good news is that reputable travel agencies rarely go out of business. The bad news is if you happened to have booked your trip through a fly-by-night travel agency, then you significantly increase the chances of something going wrong.

Before you submit your credit card number to a travel agent, there is one thing you should always check—to make sure the agency is a member of the American Society of Travel Agents or ASTA (*astanet.com*). This organization has 20,000-plus members, each of which promises to uphold a certain code of ethics. That means that you can feel confident that an ASTA-associated travel agency will treat you right—and won't leave you holding an empty honeymoon bag should they go out of business.

"If you deal with a qualified travel agency, they should not go out of business before the honeymoon," says Janet Hyman, President of Travel Duet, a national travel company based in Deerfield, Illinois. "If they decide to close their offices, a reputable travel agency will always make sure that some other travel agency takes control of their records."

For peace of mind, why not ask your travel agent this very question—What will you do if something happens to you or your office before I take my honeymoon? Find out what their Plan B is so you'll know what to expect should you see on the

6 p.m. news that the travel agency's office has burned down or you learn that the agent with whom you were working has fallen ill. With this knowledge in mind, you'll have less stress in the long run.

Finally, should something happen to the travel agent before you take your trip—and you've used a credit card to pay for your honeymoon—you may be able to dispute the charge with the credit card company and avoid paying for the trip all together. However, that does leave you without any honeymoon plans in the end, but then again, there's always *Priceline.com* for a last-minute trip or roadtrip.

Q: We called the travel agent making our honeymoon arrangements to ask her a question and discovered that she'd forgotten to book our trip. Now the resort where we wanted to stay is full. What can we do?

A: A reputable travel agent should try to make this mistake up to you, in some way possible—and don't be afraid to ask her to do so. You put your trust in this agent to book the honeymoon you wanted, and to be left without a trip is just plain wrong. I'm confident that with charter flights and tour operators at her disposal, she should be able to book you something last minute that will allow you to go away right after your wedding.

For future reference, though, you should always buy travel or trip insurance—but read the fine print, recommends Amy Ziff, Travelocity's Editor-at-Large, to make sure that the insurance will cover you if a supplier doesn't hold up her end of the bargain.

Ziff also suggests that couples be actively involved in the trip-planning process. "You want to see the confirmation plans from the hotel, airline, cruise ship, etc., so you can be rest-assured that they have left nothing to chance," she says. Case in point: I recently used a travel agent to book a weekend trip for my whole family. As I was on the phone with the agent, she faxed me a confirmation for all of our reservations. By the time I'd hung up the phone, I had a faxed confirmation in my hands and confidence that everything had been taken care of for my vacation.

If for some reason the travel agent has been withholding this information from you, you either need to press her to get proof that she's done her job, or let her know that you're going to take your business elsewhere.

Another important issue to keep in mind: Does your travel agent offer 24/7 access to well-trained customer service agents? This is especially important if you discover something has gone wrong regarding your honeymoon—and you make this discovery during nonbusiness hours.

Finally, you could call the resort at which you wanted to stay and see if they have any cancellations. However, this could be an expensive endeavor. Should the resort get a cancellation, you'll have to book a last-minute airline fare (if you're flying) to get there, and that's likely to put a huge dent in your honeymoon budget.

I think your best bet is to simply start from scratch and plan your honeymoon again. Work with a reputable travel agent who keeps you in the loop, and you're sure to have a honeymoon that won't disappoint.

Q: I saw an ad in the newspaper for a travel agent who could plan our exact same honeymoon for a cheaper price. Can I cancel with the original person?

A: I suppose you could cancel with your original person, but is the hassle really worth the money you may or may not save by changing travel agents? Also, have you read the fine print in the advertisement? Are you sure that you can get the same exact trip that you've booked for a lesser cost? Are you confident that the agency advertising this deal is a reputable firm with which to work? In all my years of traveling, I've learned this one truth with certain travel advertisements (among other things): If it sounds too good to be true, it probably is. Many times vacation advertisements are written in a way to entice customers with seemingly great deals. But once you read the fine print or learn the details, you realize that while it still may be a good deal, it isn't the good deal you thought it was.

So here's what I think you should do: Save yourself the hassle and keep your original honeymoon as is. With an entire wedding to plan, the last thing you need to do is add a level of uncertainty to your honeymoon by making a last-minute travel agent change. Stop shopping around for better bargains and just live with your honeymoon decision. You'll have less stress in the end if you stay with your original plans—especially if they're nearly or all the way complete when you stumble on this other deal.

Q: The airline we were flying to and from our honeymoon has stopped flying.

A: Sometimes airlines stop flying for good reasons, such as severe weather or mechanical problems with the planes themselves. Should you find yourself without air transportation to or from your honeymoon destination, "call the airline's customer service immediately and have them negotiate on your behalf. Be sure that you mention that it's your honeymoon—you may get some special treatment as a result," advises Amy Ziff, Travelocity's Editor-at-Large.

"If an airline files Chapter Seven bankruptcy, they will continue to fly—as has been the case recently with United, U.S. Airways, and other carriers," adds Ziff. "If the airline files for Chapter 11 liquidation, that is when flights cease." Believe it or not, though, you shouldn't fret about either scenario. Ziff says that airlines that fly the same routes as the bankrupt carrier are required to assist passengers with tickets on that route, although passengers may have to pay some sort of change-of-ticket fee. "It usually isn't much more than $25," says Ziff, who adds that these are all very good reasons to have travel insurance and to be familiar with your insurance policy—including whether or not it will cover you in the case of a bankrupt supplier, since many do not.

Ziff also recommends that you don't let dollar signs be the deciding factor in your airline choices when planning your honeymoon. In other words, you may be tempted to go with an upstart, low-cost airline that may not have an established track record, simply because it costs a lot less to fly. But think twice before booking those tickets. "It's a good idea to fly a major airline for your honeymoon trip, even if it's slightly more expensive," Ziff adds. "It's much less likely for a major airline to stop operations and cause you any worries."

Wedding Wisdom

My husband and I had just landed in the Paris airport for our honeymoon, and we were getting on a shuttle to the train station when my wallet was stolen out of my bag! The thieves were real pros. As we were getting on the shuttle a woman rudely shoved in front of me and stopped abruptly. At the same time, a man stepped in front of my husband. When I had to stop for the woman, he unzipped by bag and swiped my wallet. Because my passport was in it, we had to go to the embassy. What a hassle. It sounds obvious in retrospect, but people should make sure to keep cash, ID, passport under their clothes—special wallets are sold for travel that hang around your neck. ATM cards work just fine, even in Europe, so you don't need to carry much cash. Also, we were sleepy and distracted, but you should always be aware of who is around you in crowds. Just paying better attention would have made a difference.
—Mary, Chicago

Q: We lost our airline tickets for our honeymoon. How do I handle this?

A: Guess what? So did I. My husband and I were on our way from our reception to the airport when I realized I didn't have our tickets with us. We had our driver stop back at our house, which we tore apart looking for the tickets, but we didn't find them. Luckily, the airline had our reservation safe in their system and, after paying a $100 ticket replacement fee each, we had a new set of tickets and were on our way to our honeymoon in the United States Virgin Islands. That was back in 1993.

In today's day and age of electronic tickets, lost tickets are less of a concern for most couples. Chances are you either booked your e-ticket yourself or used a travel agent, who e-mailed or faxed you a confirmation for your flight. If you lose that confirmation, you can ask for it to be faxed to you again or you can simply print out another e-mail. However, if you paid more and requested paper tickets, you may find yourself in a situation similar to mine—paying a replacement fee for a new set of paper tickets.

If you know you're the kind of person who is likely to lose airline tickets, then I would suggest booking your flight using e-tickets. That way you can show up at the airport and use either a gate agent or the airline's computer kiosk to get your ticket. By doing so, you significantly minimize the chances that you'll misplace your tickets, and you'll erase a potential headache from your honeymoon plans.

By the way, two weeks after my husband and I returned from our honeymoon, we moved from New York to Michigan. Once we'd emptied our apartment of all of our belongings, we found our missing airline tickets—they'd fallen behind a desk and become wedged between the wall and the baseboard, which is why we couldn't find them. Needless to say we had a good laugh about it.

Q: We overslept and missed our flight. Now what?!

A: According to Amy Ziff, Travelocity's Editor-at-Large, there is no *one* answer to tell you what you can do or what will happen should you oversleep and miss your flight to your honeymoon. The first thing you should do, though, is get on the phone to the airline's customer service or speak to an agent at the airport, and play up the honeymoon mercy card. If you tell them that you got in late last night because it was your wedding night, or let them know that it was your wedding reception that somehow caused you to sleep late, the airline might just cut you some slack. "In addition, if you are a frequent flier with the airline, you'll certainly want to make sure the agent knows," she adds. "Good customers are especially important to the airline, and they always try to do right by them."

Also, a lot will depend on the kind of ticket you booked. Nonrefundable tickets offer less flexibility, so you should be prepared to pay a change-of-ticket fee—usually about $100, about the same as someone who lost his or her ticket would pay. But if you act politely and professionally when dealing with a ticket agent or customer service representative—and remind them that you're about to leave on your honeymoon—you may find a compassionate soul who will waive the fee. But this is definitely your own mistake, so go into the situation knowing that—and acting apologetic—and hopefully you'll get booked on the next flight to your honeymoon destination without too much hassle or having to pay too many extra fees.

Now that you've dealt with the airline, you've got to handle things with your resort or hotel. Here's what Janet Hyman, president of Travel Duet, a national travel company based in Deerfield, Illinois, suggests you do:

"First, call the hotel and advise them of the situation so that they do not give up your hotel room or reservation. Explain that you will work with the tour operator and rearrange flights—or will handle new arrangements on your own if you booked them directly—but most importantly, you need them to hold the room.

"Second, if your plane reservations were made through a tour operator and you have a 24/7 emergency phone contact, use it. Call the tour operator and have them try to rearrange the travel plans.

"Third, after you've called both the hotel and your tour operator, always call the travel agent and let her know what's going on. The travel agent is your advocate and will try to work with the tour operator, the hotel, and the airline to help in the rearrangement. If there was no tour operator used, and only a direct hotel booking, the travel agent will work to your best advantage."

> ### Wedding Wisdom
>
> The flight to our honeymoon destination was canceled, but we didn't find out until 90 minutes before leaving for the airport. I took a long, hot shower while my new husband booked a flight for later that day, and we were able to enjoy a last-minute, relaxing brunch with our families.
> —Diane, Virginia

Q: The airline lost our luggage and doesn't know when it might find our bags. All we have are the clothes on our back.

A: First things first: Do you have travel insurance? "A good agent will always advise a client to take trip cancellation and interruption insurance, which will cover luggage, supplier default, and illness before departure or during a trip," says Janet Hyman, President of Travel Duet, a national travel company based in Deerfield, Illinois. Also, you may want to call your insurance agent who handles your homeowner's insurance—that policy might just cover lost luggage.

While having insurance may not get your bags to you any faster, depending on the policy you choose, it will likely allow you to file for reimbursement for any clothing purchases you have to make on your honeymoon. In addition, check with your airline and see what their policy is. Once, when my husband and I went golfing in the Caribbean, our airline sent our baggage to the Bahamas by mistake. Because it would be more than 24 hours before they could get our luggage to us, they gave us a stipend (albeit a small one) to purchase an outfit, a bathing suit, shoes, and toiletries.

By the way, because airlines do lose luggage from time to time, you should always keep necessary medications in a carry-on with you. Also, if you're super-paranoid about bags getting lost, you should pack a change of clothes and your toiletries in your carry-on as well, just in case.

So definitely make sure that you buy travel insurance before any trip—especially a honeymoon—and accept the fact that if your airline loses your luggage, one of the first things you're going to have to do on your honeymoon is buy a new outfit. That's probably not the worst thing that could happen on the trip, so try to make the best of it and don't let a lost bag ruin your trip. And be sure to keep all of your receipts so that should you file for reimbursement, you have proof of what you had to buy to replace your lost luggage.

Q: Something happened and the hotel where we were staying for our honeymoon can't host us now. What are we supposed to do?

A: Whether it be that your hotel burns down, sustains damage in a storm, or closes unexpectedly, these are all reasons why it is imperative for you to have travel insurance—especially for your honeymoon. "Trip insurance is designed to protect you against unforeseen events and any of these examples would certainly count," says Amy Ziff, Travelocity's Editor-at-Large. Your insurance agent should be able to help you rebook your honeymoon or find you alternative lodging. Your travel agent should have ample options at her fingertips to allow you to find somewhere else where you can spend your honeymoon.

If you paid for your honeymoon in full and in advance, ask your travel agent to help you secure a refund from the original hotel or resort, if at all possible. If not, see if you can't dispute the already-charged fees with your credit card company.

If you didn't work with a travel agent or you can't get in touch with him or her, you should still be able to salvage the situation. " If the hotel overbooked, as happens in both Mexico and the Caribbean during prime time, they are supposed to accommodate the guests in a similar property for the night or nights that people have not checked out," says Janet Hyman, president of Travel Duet, a national travel company based in Deerfield, Illinois. "Keep calm, talk nicely, and work with the manager to see if they will accommodate you to your satisfaction."

As far as protecting yourself from any unforeseen financial emergencies, such as having to book a last-minute hotel room on your own, Hyman always advises her clients to raise their limit on their credit cards in advance of a trip. "Most credit card companies will do this with no problem," says Hyman, adding that "you should always bring an ATM card that will allow you to obtain cash in the local currency of the country you are visiting, just in case."

❧

Q: When we arrived at the hotel on our wedding night, we discovered that they'd booked us for the next night. We have nowhere to stay tonight.

A: This is exactly what happened to a client of Janet Hyman, President of Travel Duet, a national travel company based in Deerfield, Illinois. Despite having documents that confirmed the reservation for the right night, "The clients arrived in Italy, only to find that the hotel reservation was for the following night," she recalls. "Because of our 24-hour emergency service (which every good agent should have), I was able to help them. They contacted me at my home (I am the owner and they had my home number) at 4:00 a.m. our time, as it was 11:00 a.m. in Italy. Because of my company's affiliation with Virtuoso (a renowned network of luxury travel specialists), and our many personal contacts in Italy, we had the cell phone number of the correct person in Italy, who, in turn, was able to contact the manager at the hotel. Lo and behold, the manager was able to get them to clear a room, and the entire problem was solved within an hour. That is why using the right agent is the most important thing."

Not only can having a travel agent on your side help you fix this problem, but so can staying with a reputable hotel (such as a brand name you know, recognize, and trust). "A good hotel is going to do everything in their power to accommodate you or to 'walk' you to another comparable hotel nearby," says Amy Ziff, Travelocity's Editor-at-Large. She's explaining that "walking you" to another property means exactly that— that hotel personnel will "walk" you to another property that is close by. Having your room reservation get jumbled, adds Ziff, "can be unfortunate if you have been looking forward to your stay, but sometimes you can actually end up at a nicer property in a better room, and the hotel that messed up on your reservation should cover this cost for you."

Before you start demanding to be walked to another hotel, though, double-check your documents. Compare the hotel stay dates to your requests and make sure everything is arranged for the right check-in and check-out dates. It would be awfully embarrassing for you to discover that the room reservation error is your fault.

Whether you, your travel agent, or the hotel made the mistake, though, be sure to let everyone you're dealing with know that you are there on your honeymoon—this is sure to get you the best service possible. No one wants to ruin a honeymoon.

Q: Our honeymoon locale looked gorgeous in all the brochures we saw and they had a terrific Website. But when we got here, we quickly realized that it's a dump. Now we're thinking of cutting our honeymoon short.

A: The purpose of a hotel or a resort's brochure is to sell you on staying there. There's no rule that says that the brochure has to be 100-percent accurate. That's why Amy Ziff, Travelocity's Editor-at-Large, offers these suggestions when booking a honeymoon:

- Always look to friends and relatives for word-of-mouth recommendations.
- Don't judge by a brochure alone.
- Check for consumer ratings on hotels ahead of time or consult reputable rating sources to get a realistic impression of a property.

If after doing your homework you arrive and find that you are unhappy with your surroundings, quietly call your travel agent. Ask her to line up a room elsewhere, but don't commit until you know you can break your current reservation. Ziff says that you should be prepared to give up one night's stay as a penalty for canceling at the last minute, although you could ask to speak to the manager on duty, and then quietly and calmly explain the situation. See if they will let you cancel without penalty, especially because it's your honeymoon. Bottom line: Don't spend your honeymoon in a place where you're going to be miserable. Risk paying extra to change your reservation and go someplace else where you'll have a better vacation.

❦

Q: Everyone on the cruise ship we'd planned to take on our honeymoon came down with this weird virus. Should we cancel or keep our plans?

A: That is entirely up to you and how much of a risk you feel it would be to sail on that ship. Also, the cruise line may end up making the decision for you—especially if they dock that ship for decontamination, and, therefore, cancel your sailing.

Whether or not the cruise ship cancels its plan, it's likely to offer passengers like you and your new spouse the option to rebook your trip on another cruise line or to postpone travel on that ship for another date.

You may feel more comfortable booking travel on an entirely different cruise line—and one that hasn't had an outbreak of norovirus (the current term to describe the bug responsible for the outbreak of Norwalk virus on cruise ships recently). That's because the Center for Disease Control (CDC) says, "environmental contamination and infected crew members can serve as reservoirs of infection for passengers." That means that even a ship that has been decontaminated, or its crew members, could still harbor a virus that may make you sick. (Visit the CDC Website at *www.cdc.gov* for more information or to track norovirus outbreaks.)

"Cruises are very sensitive to this issue and they are taking every precaution to properly clean and sanitize ships where there are any instances of the norovirus," says Amy Ziff, Travelocity's Editor-at-Large. However, should you find yourself on a ship and there's an outbreak of norovirus, she suggests that you "wash your hands frequently and avoid eating raw and uncooked foods" to help prevent illness.

You should also look into your disembarkation options at one of your ports of call. Do so, though, only after you've checked to see if the cruise ship will reimburse you for time lost on the trip or if they'll let you take your full cruise vacation at a later date when there isn't a virus outbreak on board.

Q: My new husband ended up having an emergency appendectomy on our wedding night. Now, we can't take our honeymoon as expected.

A: This is the perfect reason to have insurance, not only for your wedding, but also for your honeymoon. For example, a company such as Access America, which provides travel protection services to millions of travelers each year, offers trip cancellation and trip interruption policies, both of which would most likely cover a honeymoon being canceled due to illness. The policy also covers someone getting sick while on vacation, and, if you pay for certain coverage, may also cover any hospitalization, medical transportation, or treatment you need or receive while you're away.

So for peace of mind about your health before and during your honeymoon, it's a good idea to secure some sort of travel insurance.

Q: I know June through October is technically hurricane season, but I figured, what are the chances of a hurricane hitting during our honeymoon? Well, it happened and now we're stranded.

A: Borrowing generously from an old TV commercial, let me say this: It's not a good idea to fool with Mother Nature. That is, if you happen to be planning a wedding during hurricane season, you would be wise to pick a honeymoon destination that is not likely to be affected by a hurricane, such as Western Canada or Europe. If you want to stay in the warmer parts of the Western Hemisphere, you may want to target the extreme southern Caribbean (such as the "ABC islands" off the coast of South America—Aruba, Bonaire, and Curacao), which usually escape the wrath of hurricanes. But, as in life, nothing is a 100-percent guarantee. That's why Janet Hyman, president of Travel Duet, a national travel company based in Deerfield, Illinois, recommends that "when hurricanes are prevalent, we will try to send honeymooners to islands that are less likely to be in the normal path of the hurricanes or we will always try to suggest cruises." Why cruises? "Because the ship will either stay in port or change directions, in order to avoid a hurricane," she explains.

If you decide to throw your honeymoon to the fate of Mother Nature and travel to a destination that could be in the path of a hurricane, be sure to invest in appropriate travel insurance that will cover you in case of bad weather.

Remember, in active hurricane years, as in 2003, you could have hurricanes making landfall on many Caribbean islands, on the east and west coasts of Mexico, on the Hawaiian islands, and as far north on the eastern seaboard as Nova Scotia, Canada, so you really do need to plan carefully and accordingly.

Q: The nation we were visiting for our honeymoon experienced a coup d'état. Now there's political unrest. What should we do?

A: In our post-September-11th world, it's not unheard of for political unrest or terrorism to cause a couple to cancel, postpone, or reconsider their honeymoon. This very thing happened in 2003 with one of Janet Hyman's clients, who happened to be planning a honeymoon that could have coincided with the war in Iraq, and it did.

"The couple really wanted to go to Greece on their honeymoon, but were afraid to book anything far ahead, due to the impending war," Hyman, president of Travel Duet in Deerfield, Illinois, recalls. "After consulting with us, they decided to book a 'safer' honeymoon to Hawaii, but opted to purchase a trip waiver should they change their mind and want to go to Greece after all. They told us that they were never told about this option from other travel agents, and were very happy to have this option available to them." Because the unrest in Iraq lasted longer than the couple expected, they did end up honeymooning in Hawaii, but they did so with peace of mind—because they had purchased travel insurance to cover any change of plans that might occur.

Travel insurance policies that work in case of war, political unrest, or terrorism aren't far-fetched notions these days. According to Amy Ziff, Travelocity's Editor-at-Large, "some travel insurance policies actually have clauses in them that allow you to postpone or cancel if terrorist events have occurred in the destination you're headed to. However, not everything is covered, so read the fine print just to be sure."

Also, understand that a travel insurance or trip interruption policy usually won't cover fear of the unknown. So if you think you might have second thoughts about vacationing in a certain location, book your honeymoon in a stable location, such as somewhere in North America where a government coup d'état isn't likely.

For additional peace of mind, check the United States State Department Website frequently during your honeymoon-planning period to see which countries appear consistently on the warning list. Then you'll know to steer clear of them as a place to honeymoon. For example, when this book was going to print, 26 countries appear on the list, including Indonesia, Iran, Iraq, and Israel.

The State Department has two warning Websites worth checking out: *http://travel.state.gov/warnings_list.html* which lists dangerous locations that currently appear on the warning list; and *http://travel.state.gov/travel_warnings.html,* which lists current worldwide dangers, including SARS outbreaks. You'll also find on this Website links to Consular Information Sheets on every country in the world. These provide basic information, such as the location of the U.S. Embassy, in case of an emergency. In addition, these sheets tell you, according to the State Department Website, "If an unstable condition exists in a country that is not severe enough to warrant a Travel Warning, a description of the condition(s) may be included under an optional section entitled 'Safety/Security.'" It's well worth any traveler's while, especially honeymooners, to check out these sites and to plan accordingly.

Finally, working with an established travel agent in planning your honeymoon can help you in a situation such as this as well. A seasoned travel agent will know how to negotiate on your behalf to book you an alternative honeymoon, or at least get you out of a trip that a political situation prevented you from taking.

Wedding Wisdom

We were married four days after September 11th, and our honeymoon flight to Bali was canceled. The State Department called U.S. citizens at the hotel we were to stay at and told them to come home. Two days later, we managed to get on a flight to Hawaii, and spent two weeks recovering from the stress of the week before, like every other American.
—Katy, Texas

Appendix

According to recent research, the average wedding in the United States costs about $20,000. That's no small drop in the bucket, and if you're paying for your wedding yourself, you obviously want to make sure that you get your money's worth from the vendors you hire. That's why I've included this Appendix that will help you find vendors that won't make you feel anxious, plus questions to ask of them and what to put in your contract with them so you won't get ripped off or end up feeling disappointed on your big day. Here are some suggestions to keep in mind:

- When searching for vendors, start by asking friends, family members, and work colleagues who they used for their weddings or special events, and which businesses they would highly recommend. Try to find at least three businesses in each area of your wedding—from bridal salon to band.

- Once you have the names of some businesses to consider, check their track record. You can do this by calling your local Better Business Bureau office or your state's Attorney General's office (which should have a consumer affairs or consumer protection division). Don't worry if you can't find any information on the businesses—that's usually a good sign and shows that people haven't filed reports against them.

- When you're ready to call businesses, be sure to get three to four estimates per specialty. By having more estimates to compare, you can see how prices and services offered differ from business to business.

- Try to target businesses that have been doing weddings for some time now. While there are plenty of new companies that could probably do a great job on your wedding, you really want to focus on a company with a track record. Most new businesses fail within their first year, so if you hire a start-up venture, you risk their going under before you ever walk down the aisle.

- Be sure to see samples of people's work, from wedding photographs of an entire wedding (not just best-of shots) to a video of a deejay's performance. When visiting a caterer, they should present you with a sample menu and let you taste some of these samples. Any caterer who doesn't want to feed you may have something to hide.

- Even though people you know referred these businesses, make sure you get two to three additional references from each business of people you don't know. Try to request couples that used the company in the last six months so they can vouch for the current personnel. Any company that is proud of its work should be happy to provide you with the names and contact information of their satisfied customers. If a business owner balks at this notion, consider that a red flag.

- Follow up with each of the references you get. Ask questions such as, "How long ago did you use this company?" and "Did you feel that you got your money's worth from this company?" and "If you could change one thing about how things went with this company, what would it be?"

- Ask to see a copy of a vendor's contract and take a copy home with you to review. Don't be afraid to ask questions about clauses or have the vendor clarify terms. You should only sign a contract that includes terms that make you feel completely comfortable.

- If the vendor doesn't have a contract to offer, find out if he'll accept a contract that you'll draw up instead. (Having an agreement in writing benefits both parties and any business owner who doesn't want to have a contract in writing is a business owner I wouldn't want to work with.) Be sure to add a clause to any contract you sign that spells out what will happen if the vendor doesn't deliver his goods or services as promised. This could be a discount on the overall price, a refund, or the offer of additional services in the future. Make sure you cover yourself against any snafu by including this kind of "responsibility" clause.

- Pay for everything and every service with a credit card. That way you have a dual safety net should something go wrong—a credit card company with which you can dispute a charge, and the Fair Credit Billing Act of 1974, which protects consumers against credit card charges for goods or services not delivered as promised.

- Confirm the details of your wedding with each of your vendors one or two weeks before your wedding, and then again two days or the day before the event. If the florist is having trouble getting the flowers you want or the band may have to substitute a musician, you'll know ahead of time and won't end up surprised on your big day.

- Bring a list of all the vendors' contact information with you on the day of your wedding. That way if there's a delay—either on your part or the vendor's part—you won't have to scramble to find their phone number.

Index

A
A.C. Moore, 163, 164, 167
acrylic nails, 33-34
airline tickets, 203-204
alcohol, 39, 144-145, 157
Ali, Asra, M.D., 23, 28
allergies, 187-189
alterations, 50, 53
American College of Nurse Midwives, 11
American Meteorology Society, 88
attendants, 69, 71-72
attendants' gifts, 72, 177-178
Attorney General's office, 74, 137, 142, 169, 170, 193, 215

B
bachelorette parties, 39
Balanced Bride, The, 9
bandleader, choosing a, 112
bar,
 cash, 154
 open, 154-157
bargain shopping,
 caterer, 143
 dress, 60
 flowers, 185-186
 invitations, 165-166
 limousines, 193-194
 rings, 191
 travel agents, 201-202
Better Business Bureau, 49, 74, 137, 142, 169, 170, 193, 215
birdhouse, wedding, 177
birth control, 11-14
 monophasic, 12
 progesterone-only, 12
 triphasic, 12
birdhouse, 177
Blue Nile, 190
bouquets, 161-162, 183, 187-188
boutonnieres, 186, 188
braces, 25
bridal attire, 57-66
Bridal Guide, 9
bridal salon, 49-50, 52, 60
bridesmaid attire, 64, 66-72
budgets, 37

C
cake-cutting ceremony, 37, 159
call sheet, 132-133
calligraphers, 170, 171
camera shyness, 125-127

cash bar, 156
caterers, 141-143
Center for Disease Control (CDS), 210
centerpieces, 186, 188-189
ceremony sites, 90-93, 97, 103,
　　104-105, 137-138
ceremony, 20, 90-91, 92, 98, 138
　　nondenominational, 95, 100
　　religious, 90-91, 92, 94-95
checks, paying with, 36-37
churches, 90-92, 93-94
comb-overs, 34
Consular Information Sheets, 213
contact lenses, 25-26, 27
contraceptives, 11-14
contracts, 74, 134, 196-197, 216-217
coworkers, 47-48
credit cards, 19, 35, 164, 207-208
cruises, 210, 211-212

D

dancing, 54
David's Bridal, 52
daylight savings, 104
deejay, 42-43, 112
　　creating a playlist for, 119-121,
　　　123-124
　　finding last minute, 122-123
　　tipping, 121-122
Depo-Provera, 12-13
dermatologists, 23-24
divorced parents, 42-46
dyeable shoes, 63

E

Elegant Wedding, 9
eloping, 41-42
emergencies,
　　beauty, 23-24
　　medical, 17, 18, 22, 39
entertainment, 38, 109-119

essentials basket, 14, 15, 54
e-tickets, 204

F

Fair Credit Billing Act of 1974,
　　35-36, 49, 61, 67, 131-132, 136,
　　164, 169, 189, 217
favors, 178-179
Federal Trade Commission (FTC),
　　35, 49, 61, 131, 189
feminine products, 14, 15
fires, 148-149, 150-151
Fishbein, Irwin H., 101
fittings,
　　for attendants, 69
　　for bride, 52-53
florists, 184-185, 186-187
flower girl, 80
flu, 17, 18
For the Bride, 9
FTC, 35, 49, 61, 131, 189

G

gift-giving practices, varying, 176
gifts,
　　attendants, 72, 177-178
　　duplicate, 174-176
glass ceremony, 107
glasses, optical, 25-26, 27
Glossary of Weather and Climate, 88
gown,
　　bridal, 49-60
　　bridesmaid, 66-67
groom's attire, 61
groomsmen attire, 72-74
guests, 38-39, 157-158

H

hairdressers, 29-32, 34
hangovers, 39-40
health emergencies, 11-22, 39

historical sites, 137-138, 146-147
honeymoons, 16-17, 200-201, 204-205, 207, 209, 211-212, 213
hotels, 207-210
huppah, 106-107
hurricanes, 88, 89, 211-212
Hyman, Janet, 199, 205-208, 211-212

I

I Do Foundation, 178
illness, coping with, 16-17, 19-20, 21, 38-39
Independent Insurance Agents and Brokers of America, 9
insects, 188-189
insurance, 200, 206-207, 211, 212-213
    wedding, 17, 52, 61, 88
interfaith marriages, 99-102
invitations, 47, 48, 164-169, 171
    ordering, 167-168

J

Jewish weddings, 107, 162
justice of the peace, finding a, 96

K

Ketubah, 102
Kinkos, 163, 164, 173
Kunin, Audrey, M.D., 23, 24, 28

L

lawyers, consulting, 36
Lewitt, Mary Jane, 11, 13
limousines, 191-197
loans, 37
luggage, lost, 206-207

M

maid of honor, 75-76, 78, 83
makeup artists, 31
makeup, 24-25, 32-33
manicures, 33-34

marriage, interfaith, 99-102
Married for Good, 178
medical emergencies, 17, 18, 22, 211
menstrual cycle, 11-14
Michaels, 163, 164, 167
money purse, losing your, 176-177

N

nails, acrylic, 33-34
National Oceanic and Atmospheric Administration (NOAA), 88
nondenominational ceremony, 91, 95, 100
norovirus, 210
Norwalk virus, 210

O

Office Depot, 164, 167, 172
OfficeMax, 164, 167, 172
officiants, 91, 92, 98-99
open bar, 156-157
open flame permit, 145-147, 155
oral surgery, 27-28
orchestra, 38
organist, 109-110

P

PaperDirect, 168
parents,
    communicating with your, 41-42, 95
    divorced, 42-44, 45-46
period, skipping your, 11-14
permit,
    alcohol, 144-145
    open flame, 145-147, 155
photographer, 125-136
    amateur, 129-130
    photojournalistic, 126
photographs, packages, 134
pimples, treating 23-24
playlist, 119-121, 123-124
Portable Wedding Consultant, The, 9

pregnancy, 15-16, 70
Priceline.com, 200
processional, 22
programs, 164-165
purse, money, losing your, 176-177

R

receiving line, 26
reception sites, 20, 141-143, 150-154
registry, 174-175
rehearsal dinner, 14-15
religious ceremony, 94-95
ring bearer, 82
rings, 189-190, 191
Rolls Royce, 192, 196
RSVPs, 166, 173-174, 180

S

sample sales, 51
sanitary products, 14, 15
SARS, 213
shoes,
    for the bride, 57, 63
    for the bridesmaids, 64
silk flowers, 188
stains, fixing, 54-56, 59
Staples, 164, 167, 172
stationer, choosing a, 163-166
Sterno, 146, 148
sunburn, treating, 28-29, 103
surgery, oral, 27-28

T

table assignments, 43
tans, 28-29
thank-you notes, 164-165, 179
tipping, 121-122
Tips for Getting a Gown in a
    Pinch, 51-52, 53, 56, 59
toasts, 160-161
transportation, 191-194

travel agency, 199-202
travel insurance, 200, 206-207, 211,
    212-213
travel safety, 213
trial runs, 31
trunk sales, 51
tuxedo rentals, 61, 72-74

U

U.S. Airways, 202
undergarments, bridal, 59, 64-66
United Airlines, 202

V

vegetarians, 149-150
videographers, 40-41, 125-133, 135-139
viruses, cruise ships, 210

W

weather, 8-9, 103-104, 211-212
Wedding Channel, 142, 184
wedding day,
    illness on your, 16-17
    rain on your, 87
wedding gift-giving practices, 175-176
wedding gown, 49-55, 57-58
    alterations, 50, 57-58
    repairing, 54-56, 59
    purchasing, 49-60
Wedding.Orders, 173
WedSafe, 52
weight, loosing and gaining, 53, 68-69

Y

Your Wedding Your Way, 106

Z

Ziff, Amy, 200, 202, 204, 207, 208,
    209, 210, 212
zits, treating, 23-24

About the Author

Leah Ingram is the author of six books: *The Complete Guide for the Anxious Bride* (New Page Books, 2004); *The Balanced Bride: Preparing Your Mind, Body, and Spirit for Your Wedding and Beyond* (Contemporary Books/ McGraw-Hill, 2002); *You Shouldn't Have! How to Give Gifts They'll Never Forget* (Contemporary Books/ McGraw-Hill, 2001); *Your Wedding Your Way* (Contemporary Books, 2000); *The Portable Wedding Consultant* (Contemporary Books, 1997); and *The Bridal Registry Book* (Contemporary Books, 1995). As a wedding, gift-giving, and etiquette expert, she is a frequent guest on many television shows. In her repeat appearances, she has either offered on-camera advice or done in-studio demonstrations for Woman's Day TV, News 12 New Jersey, News 12 Long Island, "It's Your Call with Lynn Doyle" (on the Comcast Network), along with the FOX affiliate in Detroit and the NBC, ABC, and FOX affiliates in Philadelphia.

In addition to her guest appearances, Ingram is a sought-after spokesperson and has completed national media tours for the Better Sleep Council, online jeweler BlueNile.com, spirits brand Disaronno Amaretto, Hewlett-Packard, cataloger Harry and David, the American Boxed Chocolates Manufacturers Association, and Sears. Ingram is also an editor and writer for many media outlets. She was recently a contributing editor for *Weight Watchers Magazine*, covering beauty and fashion, and acted as the interim executive editor at *Modern Bride* magazine. She was also the beauty columnist for *Philadelphia Style Magazine*.

Leah is the former editor of *Moms on Call*, an annual parenting publication from Woman's Day Special Interest Publications. She is also an accomplished journalist. Her byline has appeared in many well-known publications including *Allure, Elegant Wedding, Parade, Reader's Digest, Family Circle, Woman's Day, Bridal Guide, Islands, New York, Child, Self,* and *The New York Times*. In 2003 Ingram launched The Manners Mom, an eponymous Website (*mannersmom.com*) through which she offers advice to parents who want to raise polite children.

Ingram, who lives in Bucks County, Pennsylvania, is married and has two daughters. Check out her Website at *weddingink.com*.